STUCK
IS NOT YOUR
STORY

STUCK
IS NOT YOUR
STORY

I Overcame and Am Victorious

Stories of Victory!

Noreen N. Henry

Visionary Leader

 **VLC PUBLISHING**

Copyright © 2022
All Rights Reserved.

**Stuck Is NOT Your Story
I Overcame and Am Victorious**
by Noreen N. Henry

All rights reserved. No part of this publication may be reproduced, distributed, or transmitted in any form or by any means, including electronic, mechanical, photocopying, recording or otherwise, without prior written permission of the author. For permission, write requests to the address below.

"Scripture taken from the New King James Version©,Copyright © 1982 by Thomas Nelson, Inc. Used by permission. All rights reserved." Unless otherwise stated.

Printed in the United States of America
For information, 1803 Nereid Avenue, MB 143, Bronx, NY 10466
Victorious Living Culture
New York, NY
www.NoreenNHenry.com

Designed by Maximum Evolution
Manuscript Edited and Formatted by Maximum Evolution
ISBN

Our books may be purchased in bulk quantities for promotional, educational, or business use by churches (women's groups), associations, corporations, and all kinds of organizations.

Acknowledgments

A couple of paras are missing from the acknowledgements, here is the whole thing:

First, I thank my Divine Creator who is the leader of my life, who showed me the vision for "Stuck Is NOT Your Story" collaboration project, that I said yes to, leading me all the way.

I thank Chanel Spencer, Stuck Is NOT Your Story's" project manager. She makes it easy and seamless as we progress through the project. Chanel works diligently and tirelessly on our project, and we truly appreciate her.

I thank each co-author for joining the "Stuck Is NOT Your Story" global project, for believing in it and trusting me as the visionary leader. You are all chosen and awesome.

Since the first book in the series "Stuck Is NOT Your Story: Change Is Possible" in 2021, we have been fortunate to see our book used by professional organizations. I send special thanks to those that are using our book "Stuck Is NOT Your Story" for a purpose. The book clubs, the counselors, therapists and coaches to help their clients. Stuck Is NOT Your Story's mission is to impact millions of people in a positive way and by you using it in this capacity is helping us to reach our goal.

We thank each reader in advance for reading each story with compassion and empathy to see that it is possible to overcome to victory, become unstuck to live your best life NOW, and that is victorious living.

Dedication

Stuck Is NOT Your Story: I Overcame and Am Victorious is dedicated to our Divine Creator who is the head of the "Stuck Is NOT Your Story" collaboration project.

Second, it's dedicated to you that have suffered through trials and tribulations that caused you to become broken and/or stuck to show you that you are not alone and that you too can overcome and be victorious. It is possible for lasting change because "Stuck Is NOT Your Story" and victorious living is possible.

Note To Reader

We all go through different circumstances in our lives that can keep us broken and stuck, but we don't have to stay there. Most of the times we remain broken or stuck is due to not having the right knowledge, Hosea 4:6 says we perish for lack of knowledge.

Sometimes we don't even know that we are broken or stuck. It is in the NOT accepting the defeat of the circumstances and in doing something different that we overcome brokenness and become unstuck.

Let's all do something different so that we can be overcomers and live victoriously.

Noreen N. Henry
Visionary Leader

Trauma is a universal wound not everyone overcomes.

This is a book about those who do and the inspiration they provide to others.

How do you handle your nightmare scenario? Do you curl into a ball and wait for the storm to pass? Do you take control of your situation? Even though you know doing so might cause you pain because deep down inside you know it is the only way to escape and rebuild your life?

Stuck is NOT Your Story: I Overcame and Am Victorious is a compilation of seemingly impossible stories where women from all walks of life are forced to do the unthinkable, to dig deep within themselves and rise above their trauma, reforged into who they want to be and who they deserve to be.

This awe-inspiring group of stories will leave you shaking your head, wondering how these women managed to grow from their issues. It is a testimonial to the rest of us. A wake-up call proclaiming that we do not have to settle. There is a better day, and it is ready for the taking.

Contents

Acknowledgments v

Dedication vii

Note To Reader viii

Preface xiii

Foreword Erica Latrice xv

Introduction 19

Destruction to Reconstruction 23
    Dr. JoWanda Rollins-Fells

Shattered Confidence? Never Again! 35
    Carol M. Quigless

A Brave Heart 41
    Marilyn Green

Becoming Light After Loss 45
    Shontae Horton

I Choose Joy 53
    Joy Green

It Tried to Kill Me, But I Landed on My Feet! 63
    Andrea Briscoe

Not Built To Break 73
    Lynnecia S. Eley

Army Strong Built Ford Tough 81
    Tracey Ford

Had to Choose Me 93
    Nicole Rhone

Overcome F.E.A.R. to R.I.S.E. 103
    Latika Vines

Stuck Is Not My Story, I Overcame (Playing the Victim) 113
    Priscilla C. Baldwin

Unstuck from Emotional Eating and Food Addiction 125
    Noreen N. Henry

Acknowledgements 141

Preface

"Stuck Is NOT Your Story: I Overcame and Am Victorious" is a global movement of courageous stories shared by vulnerable women who overcame topics of serious illnesses, wanting to give up, losing a child, plus more, to show that you are not alone and that you too can overcome and be victorious to live the life of your dreams. This is also to encourage, inspire, and impart knowledge and wisdom.

This book "Stuck Is NOT Your Story: I Overcame and Am Victorious" is the second one in the "Stuck Is NOT Your Story" series.

Stuck Is NOT Your Story: I Overcame and Am Victorious is for you to know that you are not alone, that you too can overcome and be victorious, or help you see that you are stuck or broken and can do something about it. We all go through different trials and tribulations and some of them do have us broken and stuck. For instance, I was stuck in the cycle of emotional eating that progressed to a bad relationship with food and I developed bad eating habits. It took me years before I became unstuck, and it was due to gaining the right knowledge. There are many things that we can be stuck in. For example, unhealthy relationships, unhappy in the job, an illness, addictions, etc. The list can go on and on.

The Stuck Is NOT Your Story compilation of stories is to motivate and inspire you to take the necessary steps needed for change, and it takes courage to do. You don't have to stay stuck or broken, and you are the one, individually, that has to do something different to have the change you want to see in your life. As the Word says, "faith without works is dead" (James 2:26).

Foreword
Erica Latrice

I am honored for the opportunity to share why the message of "Stuck Is NOT Your Story" is so important. I have personally experienced seasons in my life where it seemed that things would never look up. Having experienced setbacks and challenges I know how vital it is to lean on support and wisdom to overcome. I remember losing most everything that I owned at one point due to a natural disaster. As I looked around and assessed all that was gone I understood in the moment, the power of having a support system and the impact of being surrounded by others. I was able to not allow that moment to define where I would be because of my trust in God and the people around me. I now speak to thousands of women around the world with a message of hope and inspiration. Having spoken on national stages and being a featured expert in top media publications around the world as a PR & Media Strategist, it has been clear to me that success is not just defined by your achievements but how we are able to continue in the face of what seems like adversity.

I know how messages like Stuck Is NOT Your Story can be the very thing that we need to hear in times of preparing for triumph. A message of overcoming is truly a decision, Many people face setbacks and often take it as an indication to give up. Noreen however has seen her setbacks as an opportunity to give back and pour into others. Being able to glean from others who have overcome trials is one of the most effective and powerful ways to move beyond your own challenges. Having observed the Victorious Living movement that Noreen has led overtime I know that she truly stands on the message of overcoming challenges. From dealing with eating disorders, to pushing past fears she has been on a consistent mission to help others remove the blocks in their lives to get unstuck. She is truly an example of what it means to not allow your limitations to define where you have the ability to go in life.

It is a privilege to share how this book is going to make a difference in the lives of so many readers. Having spent 10+ years in media and marketing and working with several hundred authors I know when something is created from a place of true passion. This book was written from a place of wanting to see change and joy in the lives of others and I believe that it will do just that! The day that you decide that stuck is no longer your story is the day that things can begin to change. When you are ready for that change it is crucial to begin to surround yourself with the stories and support of others who have made that same decision.

If you are dealing with adversity it is important to understand that you can and will overcome when you make the decision to do so! Stuck Is NOT Your Story!

Erica Latrice
Speaker, Author & Media Host

Erica Latrice

Erica Latrice is on a mission to help you understand your purpose and live the life that God has created you to live! She has been featured in The Huffington Post, Prevention, Woman's Day and many other media outlets empowering others to stop playing small and start living their dreams!

She is a Speaker, Published Author and has served as a media expert on platforms alongside some of the top producers in television, radio and print media worldwide.

This is more than a career; Erica's tenacity, spiritual walk and commitment to your success are the driving force behind her company *Be Inspired! Inc. and her work as a **Speaker, Founder & Mentor** with the **AmplifyHER Movement**.* Her TV show has aired in more than 17 million U.S. Households and is growing worldwide. Her Passion is truly helping others to realize their potential and live a purpose-filled life!

Her Faith:

Erica dedicated her life to Jesus while attending college. She credits this to the biggest turning point in her life! Surrendering her ideas and plans and allowing God to direct her steps opened doors that she never imagined. She is most dedicated to helping others know Jesus as the Lord & Savior of their lives. She is determined to be a tremendous blessing in the lives of her family, friends and anyone that she has the opportunity to cross paths with.

Get connected Facebook: @EricaEmpowers | Twitter @EricaEmpowers | Instagram @EricaEmpowers | Youtube @EricaEmpowers | Periscope @EricaEmpowers

Introduction

"It's not death that man should fear, but fear never beginning to live."

~Marcus Aurelius

Do you know that many Americans are quite unhappy? And that some don't know that they are unhappy because of their lives being the norm.

The Washington Post has an article titled: *"Americans are getting more miserable, and there's data to prove it."* This article was written in March 2019. We have to work on changing that.

The Happiness index says: *"Only 1 in 3 Americans are very happy"* according to the Harris Poll. We have to work on changing this too.

But, there is always hope for real, lasting positive change as we gain the right knowledge.

There was a young lady (about 18 years of age) who met a young man and fell in love with him believing that she would be with him for the rest of her life.

As usual, the beginning of a relationship is great.

The relationship was going well and a few years into it, things began to change, and not in a good way.

The man started being emotionally abusive. The lady stayed with the man believing that he would change and be how he was in the beginning years.

She stayed in the relationship, married the man, and had children with the man.

After all this, things got worse. The verbal abuse was happening daily. The lady began to feel bad about herself. She knew the things he would say weren't true, but she would second guess herself at the same time, and she still believed the man would change to how he used to be, so she continued in the relationship. She was very unhappy; she even lost her true self.

The faces we wear, no one knew she was so unhappy in her relationship. No one knew she was being verbally abusive. At the time, she didn't know that what he was doing was abusive.

The last straw for her was when he had relations with another women. She couldn't do it anymore. She left the relationship and began to get back to herself.

Since then, she has been doing very well.

If she had stayed in the relationship, who knows what would have happened. Firstly though, she would still be unhappy, waiting for the man to change for the better. And, she would still be feeling bad about herself.

This is just a tid bit of this story, but can you imagine being in a relationship where you go around the same mountain day in day out and year in year out, expecting things to change without doing anything different.

This story shows why it is important to gain the right knowledge. But it's not only to gain the right knowledge, but to apply it to your life. Gaining and using the right knowledge is key.

If this lady had the right knowledge on how to deal with the verbal abuse and not fall victim to it, she would have lived a happier life at a much younger age. She would have had a victorious life staying in continual joy, peace, and happiness.

This lady was broken and stuck while in the relationship. She endured heartache and pain because of not knowing how to deal with the situation back then.

It is extremely important to gain the right knowledge, and to also do something different to not be stuck in circumstances that cause us to be broken and end up being stuck.

Are you broken or stuck in circumstances and want real, lasting change?

As you read the overcomer stories of victory in this book, let them be an encouragement to you to know that you are not alone, and that you too can overcome in your life issues to victory as well.

Victorious living, it's possible!

CHAPTER 1
Destruction to Reconstruction
Dr. JoWanda Rollins-Fells

Within the pages of "Stuck is Not Your Story", you will find a safe place to hear about the vulnerabilities of others and how they have overcome them. Some stories you will identify with, and other stories will make you grateful that you did not journey that same path. While reading this book, you are free to be honest with yourself and release whatever has you stuck. Turn destruction into reconstruction and live your victorious life.

A Peek Inside the Destruction.

My heart dropped like a boulder with the force of a million tons, taking down everything in its path.

The avalanche was followed by an arctic wind that chilled my veins. I was reduced to a hollow cavity kept together by a network of icy sludge that barely chugged along. A coldness registered in my senses as the warmth left me.

The shell of my body created an echo of silence that rang loud in my ears. Whispers of those around me and my own thoughts filled the void. It was hard to breathe under the pressure of these conditions.

The once vivid and colorful thoughts that swirled in my imagination were becoming eclipsed by a thick dark cloud that lingered. The zest and zing of thriving in life began to flatline in a hum of static that occasionally picked up reception.

Meanwhile, my voice was choked out by the lack of strength and energy to push forward the air necessary to make audible sounds.

My mind was still firing rapidly though. I was consciously aware that no one could see what I was feeling or thinking.

When I whispered for help, those around me were not discerning the weakness in my voice or the pleading in my eyes. Even if I yelled as loud as I could, I was aware that no one would really hear me. So, to avoid adding further insult to injury, I remained quiet. Quiet, because I didn't want those around me to fail to answer my call or to feel guilty for not knowing what to do. Furthermore, to even ask for help would somehow insinuate that what I was enduring was worthy to be considered significant in the realm of all of the tragedies in the world.

I chose silence. Silence, out of integrity to the perception of people. Silence, because I did not have words to articulate how I was feeling or what I needed.

I justified my silence by wrapping it in a banner of endurance.

Suffering was a sign of strength, or so my warped sense of reality tried to justify. This ill-informed logical fallacy, whispered for me to SUCK IT UP like everyone else has to. It was just my turn to suffer. So, I trudged forward with the mission to simply endure.

The bomb that triggered the internal destruction was real. The damage was real. The hurt was real. The silence was even more real. Being trapped inside yourself is a hard place to be stuck.

Stuck is Not Your Story. You are an Overcomer.

Were you able to see and feel what I just described? Were you able to relate? For some of you, reading "A Peek Inside the Destruction" may feel like the rejection you are facing. Perhaps, it feels like the depression or anxiety that you are battling with. Perhaps, a negative doctor's report or diagnosis makes the words relevant to you. Maybe you are reading this chapter and you don't even know why you understand "A Peek Inside the Destruction", but you do.

Let me assure you that, however you connect with the text, there is a message in this chapter for you to rebuild. *Stuck is NOT Your Story; You are an Overcomer and are Victorious.*

As Noreen Henry, the visionary leader of this anthology says, **"Let's get equipped with the right knowledge."** Let's begin to gain freedom by talking about the lies that deceive us and the rules that restrict us and keep us stuck.

The Lies that Deceive Us: Logical Fallacy

Reasoning that comes to a conclusion without evidence to support it; a false or mistaken idea.

So much of what we build on the inside of us is subject to creation based on logical fallacies. The stuck place happens when we accept these flawed arguments as truth and allow them to rule our lives. Here are a few examples:

We experience something in a relationship with a man and then come to believe that all men have the same tendencies. Maybe he is not exhibiting it currently, but the capacity to lie and cheat is there. So, it is not a matter of IF he will be unfaithful, but rather a question of WHEN he will cheat. Seriously, if Jay-z can cheat on Beyonce, then none of us are safe. All men are cheaters. Logical Fallacy.

We experience betrayal in our female circle of friends, and we believe that a group of women can't get together without jealousy and cat fights occurring. So, we keep our circles small, don't overlap circles of friends, and cut off anyone who even looks like they will offend us. Seriously, you can turn on any reality TV show and be entertained by the chaos. Women just can't get along. Logical Fallacy.

We experience conflicts with business, because people don't hold up their end of the bargain. So, get what you came for, and you will never leave disappointed. It's a dog-eat-dog world. Seriously, people can't be trusted even with a signed contract. There is no such thing as collaboration, only competition. Logical fallacy.

Your family will only support you, when there is something of benefit to them. So, don't expect them to share in your struggles, but do be prepared to bless them in your abundance. It is selfish, if you don't share. Logical fallacy.

These are all LOGICAL FALLACIES that we have heard so many times that we believe that they are ABSOLUTE truths! I can think of an incident for every example given and a time where these experiences caused me to feel the hurt described in "A Peek Inside the Destruction".

Just because these situations have happened doesn't mean that it is ALWAYS true and true about EVERYONE.

So, how do we overcome logical fallacies?

1. Try not to speak in terms of "Always, Never, Nothing, and Nobody".
2. Pray for discernment to understand what we are dealing with and how to handle it.
3. Be flexible in our thinking to assign the correct reasoning in order to come to the right conclusion.
4. Learn from the times where the argument is proven to be true and recognize when we have contributed to the situation ourselves.
5. Trust with wisdom until trust is broken.

The reality is that every relationship is NOT wrought with infidelity. Women are often the heartbeat of a thriving ecosystem of empowerment. Collaboration and integrity in business builds a table that has enough room for everyone to eat from. The lack of family presence does not necessarily equate to a lack of support.

Don't let the logical fallacies that you have experienced stifle you in life. Release the arguments that are just not true. Release the line of thinking that only keeps you bound inside and hurt.

Trust is a simple gift with a profound reward. Trusting with wisdom means that we ask God for discernment, so that we know in which ways to trust and in which ways to protect ourselves. We are often taught that trust is to be earned and not given. I am learning to extend trust as a baseline gift that is to be maintained; rather than a status based on the debts of others to be earned. It allows me to reframe relationships as one of abundance instead of a place of lack.

This is admittedly easier in words than in action because of our paradigms, which are the rules that restrict us to auto-piloted responses.

Paradigms: The Rules that Influence Our Behavior

The logical framework that we build about life guides our thoughts and perceptions. That is why we must address the logical fallacies. Next, we must address the way we ACT in response to what we believe. This is where a conversation about our paradigms comes into place. Our paradigms can restrict us and limit our choices of how to behave and respond. Limited choices can lead to stuck places.

Paradigms are stubborn and do not want to change. They are embedded so deeply within us, that we are often not aware of them, unless we are challenged to think about them. They help us to justify WHY we do what we do and HOW we do it. Let's give it a try by seeing if you can complete the following sentences and see if we recognize some of the same paradigms.

If you hit me then, I can …… (hit you back).
Sweep off your own front porch before you …… *(try to clean off mine)*.
If you don't have anything nice to say …… *(say nothing at all)*.
You scratch my back, and I will …… *(scratch yours)*.
A dog that will bring a bone will ……. *(carry a bone)*.
Snitches get ……. *(stitches)*.
Burn me once then shame on you. Burn me twice ……. *(shame on me.)*

While that was a harmless activity, what about when the paradigms are destructive, abusive, or racist?

When you combine logical fallacies and fixed paradigms, you often get a STUCK PLACE.

Let me explain.

My paradigms are present in the excerpt from my original writing "A Peek Inside the Destruction", where you can see and feel the STUCK PLACE because…

1. I expect ME out of other people. (Read that again slowly.)
2. The audacity of situations often takes me by surprise and causes an avalanche of emotions.
3. Instead of lashing out, I tend to become guarded and emotionally disconnected to cope.

4. I struggle with asking for help.
5. My silent inner turmoil is over my worthiness as compared to others.

So how do we overcome our paradigms?

First, we have to acknowledge that we do have paradigms that can be the puppet masters of our behavior. As you read this book, I encourage you to take note of your reactions and connections to the stories. You are most likely connecting because your paradigm connects.

Second, recognize that paradigms can change with new information and new habits. Instead of being surprised by the audacity of a situation, I have learned to take away the shock value. Limiting the shock of a situation limits the avalanche of emotions for me. I have also learned to be free from the "always and never" logical fallacy and live more in the mindset that "It is what it is, and it is not what it is not."

I expect honor, respect, and loyalty in situations. However, I released the paradigm of expecting people to act or respond the way that I would in a situation. They are not ME. So, how was that realistic in the first place? It sounded good though.

Now that we have identified logical fallacies in our framework and destructive paradigms that govern our behavior, let's be free!

With new information comes new responsibility - the responsibility to rebuild.

"A Peek Inside the Reconstruction"

I trudged forward with the mission to endure. I began to whisper the logical fallacy that I had accepted as truth; it was my turn to suffer, and suffering was a sign of strength. My paradigm said I should endure the struggle with great pride and be the master of my own fate. It encouraged me to not think so highly of myself as to ask for help or to deem myself worthy of the help that I needed.

I walked around with my heart sunken at the betrayal that I received from people whom I loved. The cunning antics, that stole from me what I was willing to freely give, solidified the ice in my veins. I turned off all emotional capacities to care because caring made me vulnerable. I didn't want to serve people anymore, because I was tired of being mentally and emotionally plundered.

I looked around at the destruction, and I felt shame. Shame is anger turned inward. and I felt ashamed that I knew this psychological truth because I train this truth as a consultant.

To break the silence, I began to engage in debates with God about why he made me the way that He did. Why a visionary and champion for people? Why was I required to care for people who were now throwing rocks and hiding their hands? People who were whispering about it being my turn to fail, since life had previously been so good to me. Jeers about my faith that God would see me through were now comfortable comments to make in my presence as if I was deaf and blind.

I was tired, worn, exhausted, and overwhelmed. I was ready to either give in or go down with a fight. A fight playing by the rules of my paradigm, before I gave my life to Christ. The paradigm that gave me the right to hit you back, get what I came for, and go for the jugular. I wanted to ignore the saved paradigm of the turn the other cheek with an allowance for righteous indignation.

As much as I would like to say that I was hardcore and ruthless in my inner gangster; the truth was that through it all, I was keenly aware that I was being kept. Kept by God himself who was guarding against my demise.

My spirit was keeping me when my mind and my body were failing. My spirit was somehow surviving in the aftermath of my emotional avalanche. At times it sparked its way around the neural pathways of my brain and ignited a thought or prayer. It would send shocks to my heart to keep the pulse and the warmth that melted the icy sludge in my veins. My spirit was an ember of energy to my feet to keep trudging along and a light that shone on the path in which I was to walk.

Every day, I began to look for something good in the things around me and was amazed at how much we overlook in our busy schedules. The stars always shone with beauty and amazement, and the portrait of the sunrise and sunset never ceased to amaze me. Nobody could paint all of the infinite possibilities that occurred with the wisp of the wind. God was challenging my framework and paradigms by challenging how I used the words "always, nothing, never, and nobody". God was gentle with me in helping me to recognize that everything I needed to reconstruct what I thought was broken, was already inside of me.

He gave me my breath back first by opening my airways with a fresh anointing in my nostrils. Breathing in and out supplied my body with the oxygen needed to think clearly. Next, He addressed my thoughts. Who said I was suffering? Since when did what people say about me override what He said about me? Why did I allow my own voice to harmonize with the off-key notes of others? He held me and patted my back like a baby until I was ready to clear my throat and expel the toxic gases that filled my lungs. I found my voice in a whispered prayer or song of worship.

He fortified my heart with by stitching purpose as my anchor and hiding His Word in the creases. He gave me a blood transfusion that cleared the sludge and sealed me with His holy covenant. He shocked me back to life and discharged thoughts that were not His thoughts and set up a new paradigm where my ways were like His ways.

When it was time to test my new hearing, he shook me up like you shake a jug of orange juice. He turned me upside down so that things would get back in order and alignment. He opened my eyes to see that my spirit and His spirit were intertwined like a gifted bow. So that when He moved, I moved. He was the keeping force and not me.

God opened my eyes to see that part of the calling of ministry is to see hurts so that I could minister to them, and not to become them or to be overwhelmed by them. God revealed the trick of the enemy to wear me down and overtake me in sensitive places. He reminded me that He has pulled back the curtain so that I could see what was going on inside because He desired me to be an active participant in rebuilding and overcoming.

He whispered these words to me:

"You are exactly who I say that you are. Although you may have doubted yourself, I have never doubted you. Trust me when I say that no weapon formed against you shall prosper. You have nothing, but rather gained wisdom, insight, and compassion that will enable you to continue to serve. Guard your heart and your mind. I have seen your obedience to Me, and it is far greater than any sacrifice. The time has come to rise from the ashes. There is beauty awaiting you every day with the rising of the sun and the going down of the same. My glory abides with you like the song of the birds. You are blessed because I say that you are. Now, arise, go. There is much to be done."

I say to you, the reader, know that you have been equipped with everything you need. Embark on the journey of understanding what you have been given and how to use it.

Remind yourself of Jeremiah 29:11 – "For I know the plans that I have for you", declared the Lord, "plans to prosper you and not to harm you, plans to give you hope and a future."

Fight for your hope! Fight for your future!

Fight to not only survive, but fight also to thrive!

Stuck is Not Your Story, you are an OVERCOMER! Live your VICTORIOUS LIFE!

Dr. JoWanda Rollins-Fells

Dr. JoWanda Rollins-Fells is a highly respected inspirational keynote speaker, ordained minister, and skilled consultant. She is affectionately known as "Dr. Real Talk", and her mission is to help people around the world through the framework of **R**eframing reality; **E**mpowering vision; **A**ctivating faith; and **L**iberating legacy.

She wears many professional hats, as she leverages her experience and expertise across the fields of education, public speaking, and media production.

Her journey of empowering others began in the hallways of k-12 public education as a National Certified teacher and leader for 15 years. She ran for public office and began her term on the local School Board in 2014. In 2020, Dr. Rollins-Fells was elected to serve as the Eastern Region Chair representing 15 school boards in Virginia. This experience is evidence of her champion spirit and commitment to issues facing children, families, teachers, and communities.

As an educational consultant, Dr. Rollins-Fells trains and empowers school divisions and social service agencies across the United States of America as they interface with at-promise populations. Her training topics include "A Framework for Understanding Poverty", "Bridges Out of Poverty", and "Emotional Poverty."

As an inspirational speaker, Dr. Rollins-Fells is a passionate presenter who builds the case for walking in unencumbered freedom through the R.E.A.L. framework previously mentioned. She is the award-winning author of "Stuck Is Not Your Story; Change is Possible", which was featured in New York Times Square and "Employee to Empire", "Marketing and Branding", and "Affirmations of a CEO on the Move".

She is the CEO of Spirit of Excellence LLC, where she provides coaching and a full suite of marketing platforms to authors, speakers, coaches, and ministers who are serious about the work of empowering others and want to increase their reach and visibility. Spirit of Excellence Media, Power of One Ministries, Power of One Magazine, and Power of One Radio are all part of the suite of media solutions that Dr. Rollins-Fells leverages in support of her mission.

She is a proud graduate of Hampton University and Capella University, where she has been equipped with multiple degrees including a Ph.D. that have provided her with an understanding of people, processes, motivation, and transformation.

Dr. Rollins-Fells is a wife, mother and minister who humbly thanks God for giving her the wisdom and strength for the legacy she is living and the legacy she is building to extend for generations.

CHAPTER 2
Shattered Confidence? Never Again!
Carol M. Quigless

I nearly gave up my career as a massage therapist, because I lost my confidence in my ability to be effective. It was a couple of years after I had trained in Russian Medical Massage. The training was rigorous and demanding. The book learning required studying anatomy, physiology, and the energy dynamics of muscle tone and movement or kinesiology. We studied the workings of the myofascia plus the interplay and connectedness of muscle groups. The hands-on practice involved many hours. It exposed us to different kinds of muscle conditions.

At first, the class practiced various massage techniques on each other, and then later on, with the public at large under the close scrutiny of our mentor, Boris Prilutsky. He made sure we followed protocol for the best results from preparing first the muscles to relax before receiving manipulation with the end result of relief from pain.

After all the intense training and practice, I was confident and ready to take on the problems of pain and restricted movement that I expected to be presented with from clients. Sometimes, relief from pain and tightness would happen immediately, and other times, it would take a few sessions, depending on underlying conditions. My clients were pleased, and I was happy with the work and the results. It seemed I had a natural affinity for the work.

I then got a call from a man named Dan, who had heard about my work via word of mouth. His wife, Liz, was suffering from an incurable degenerative nerve condition, and he thought massage might help. I agreed to drive an hour and a half to their house to see what I could do, armed with all my knowledge, practice, and essential oils. When I arrived at the house, Dan welcomed me at the door with a wide smile, his two children in tow with faces filled with cautious curiosity. He led me to a room, where Liz was sitting on a bed. She was an attractive woman but her face was expressionless, which I was not prepared for.

Liz's condition was advance – her neck and shoulders were frozen in an awkward position. Her musculature was rigid and had a leather-like quality throughout her body. I had not seen this advance condition in my massage school training. Liz was unable to speak but could peck out short phrases on a keyboard. This let me know that there was plenty of life and engagement going on behind the mask-like quality of non-expression. I took all this in, took a deep breath, and then set about her massage. I felt the vast amount of damage that the disease had caused, the rigidity, the tightness. Muscles that were meant to be supple were taut like steel cables and no doubt painful. This scenario gave me pause. After understanding the severity of Liz's condition, I still thought that somehow, I could bring about some relief, some progress.

After four sessions with Liz, there was some improvement but far too little. The muscles in her neck were not as tight to the touch but still taut and twisted. The rigidity throughout her body persisted. I had no doubt she was in pain in spite of medication. After a couple more sessions, I realized that great progress was not to be had. But I was not one to give up, and Dan insisted on the massage sessions. He felt that they were helping. However, I felt so absolutely sad for Liz, for her pain and deterioration. I had never dealt with incurable progressive terminal conditions before. I also felt so absolutely sad for Dan and the children standing by and seeing Liz's pain and deterioration. They knew she would not recover, that the end was nearing. I grew to feel inadequate, defeated, and helpless. I had heretofore always brought relief and any relief I brought to Liz seemed minor. Finally, after one of the sessions, I felt devastated and I cried the whole long drive home. Loud wracking sobs just kept coming from me. I was ready to quit my massage practice. Although I had continued seeing other clients while dealing with Liz, I was fixated on her situation. I felt as though this was a test, and I failed to be effective. I was used to getting results and sometimes very dramatic ones. Dan was always glad to see me when I arrived, but I didn't see where I was doing much good. This was a family of good, nice people working hard and absolutely rooting for Liz. I could do nothing much. I lost confidence. And cried.

I couldn't think straight and felt hopeless. I sought advice from a very wise person about this situation. First thing, he emphatically said, "Don't give up!" I was surprised because I felt like such a failure. He went on to say that it was true, I could not cure Liz. The "cure" is usually the criteria, the verdict on whether or not one has succeeded. There is the expression I've heard in medical settings, "I can't do anything for her, let's just keep her comfortable," which is the equivalent of "I couldn't cure her, I can't help her." That was my conditioning, as I came from a medical family.

My Dad was a legendary general practitioner in rural North Carolina, and my brother was a surgeon. For them the measure of success was clear. Yet my mentor went on to say the healing takes place in different ways – on the emotional level, on the spiritual level, with the ability to forgive, the ability to receive or give love, and more. In short, the practice of healing comes from the heart. These aspects of the human condition are different for each one of us, and the need for healing takes on urgency as we face mortality. My mentor went on to explain that I was actually doing very well with Liz. He said that I was so sad and despondent, because I had made a connection with Liz and my heart was opening. He said my desire to help Liz was genuine and that Liz would receive that as compassion. Compassion works wonders. My massage touch with my special oils, my attentiveness and compassion were acts of healing. I did not quite understand what he was talking about because I had not considered my work through massage and essential oils as anything other than relief for my clients on a surface level. I had not thought about the impact it could have on emotional or spiritual levels. Nevertheless, this wise soul advised me to go back and continue working with Liz and that this situation was indeed a lesson – a lesson that all healers must go through. That I really did not understand: me, a healer? I had never considered myself to be a healer. I was not even trying to be a healer. I did not have a concept of what that meant.

I took this wise person's advice. I went back for another session with Liz. As usual, Dan met me at the door and welcomed me in. I went over to assess how Liz was doing, and nothing much had changed. Rigidity was still there, and her face was expressionless. I took a deep breath, as I usually did before starting a massage. Before I placed my hands on her, Liz started typing on her keyboard, "I love Ca…." Then she stopped. She erased it and typed, "I love massage." Dan chuckled and seemed very pleased at this, smiling broadly. I was totally astonished! It was as if this scenario had been scripted, but it was not. Out of the blue, Liz spontaneously typed this! It was her way to show appreciation and to say "thank you" to me. What I could not see previously was that Liz experienced my touch, special oils, attentiveness, and genuine desire to help as healing, and my compassion mattered. This brought her relief, as she was living through her final days. I was so moved by this and glad that she loved my being there to help her. I was also humbled to my very core. I felt that my heart was wide open and ready to give without hesitation, with the knowledge that this was a good, healing thing. I composed myself from the shock of this occurrence and moved close to work on Liz, viewing her from a new perspective. Yes, her muscles were still taut and her neck and shoulders still twisted. But I now approached her with new energy and faith that my touch and special essential oils brought her a sense of relief on other levels.

In spite of my inability to cure, I had a way to bring compassion, comfort, relief, love and a bit of joy to someone, who was suffering and terminally ill. I saw that I was able to bring comfort to Liz's family as well. Dan and the kids saw that Liz loved being worked on, and this brought them some relief and comfort, too. Again, I cried all the way home but this time out of gratitude and humility.

It was only a short time later that Dan called to let me know that Liz had passed away. Although grieving, he knew he had done all he could to ease her transition. I felt the same way.

After my experience with Liz and her family, I was able to help others in much the same way and without doubting myself or my purpose at hand. There was the eight-year-old girl, who was dying at home. Her mother called me, and I worked on her with special essential oils to bring her peace of mind. I showed her mother how to use the oils and how to gently massage. It was years later at a social gathering that the little girl's mother saw me and rushed to hug me, thanking me for bringing her some ease and her daughter.

There was the elderly man, who only had days to live. His wife called me, because he was in so much pain despite medication. I was able to bring him some relief, and he said the massage was the only thing that worked. He said this with a smile of gratitude. There was the terminally ill woman dying in bed at home. Her thirteen-year-old daughter would watch me intently, as I helped her mother out with massage and special essential oils. A few months after her mother died, she asked if she could apprentice with me to find out about the oils that were so comforting. In a similar way, an adult daughter and sister of a terminal cancer client found inspiration while witnessing massage, Reiki and aromatherapy that the client received. That brought them comfort that helped sustain them during their grieving. I had learned that it is not enough to be a clinician. Compassion or heart connection is necessary in all situations, where healing is involved. And it is not reserved only for those facing death but also for those desiring to embrace life and need assistance through healing on various levels. I speak of the man battling crippling depression where compassionate body/energy work plus aromatherapy aided a breakthrough in his ability to cope with life. I also speak of the man who hobbled in pain to his first session with me and who did not really expect a good outcome. He received energy work and aromatherapy in a calm caring environment. He told me later that he felt so good that he played three games of Squash afterwards. I was shocked! I would not have advised that he do that but all went well.

So my mentor was right. When I started working with Liz, I was thrown into the midst of learning a lesson about healing. I'm so glad I did not give in to my shattered confidence. Because I rose to the challenge of regaining my confidence, I continued to garner more knowledge, not only about my craft but also about the human spirit. I was inspired to deepen my knowledge about the healing properties of essential oils and became a Certified Clinical Aromatherapist. I felt compelled to learn about energy work and became a Reiki Master-Teacher. I never stopped learning about these things and massage modalities. I got my confidence back, and it created a ripple effect, touching many people in positive ways. I learned my lesson and never looked back. Stuck is not my story!

"Compassion works wonders!"

Four tips for living:

1. Never be ashamed of your tears.
2. Take 3 long deep breaths in the morning, afternoon, and evening.
3. Let laughter be a daily habit.
4. Cultivate gratitude. It may be your guiding light in your darkest hour.

Carol M. Quigless

Carol M. Quigless was born in the rural town of Tarboro, NC. As an adult she lived in New York City and Los Angeles before settling in the Blue Ridge Mountains in Charlottesville, VA. She is a Board Certified Massage Therapist, Certified Clinical Aromatherapist, and Reiki Master-Teacher. Ms. Quigless has a private practice in Charlottesville and presents workshops for both the general public and bodyworkers. She also teaches all levels of Reiki. Ms. Quigless is dedicated in educating people about natural health modalities to assist them in developing healthy lifestyles.

Ms. Quigless previously opened a natural healing clinic in Tarboro, NC, which offered massage, clinical aromatherapy, and Reiki on a sliding fee scale. The area hospital and health department tapped her to present healthy cooking lessons, drawing on her experience as a private chef to Hollywood luminaries while living in Los Angeles. She currently has an aromatherapy company, Flourish Essential Oils, where she has created over 30 formulas to help the body heal physically, emotionally and spiritually.

Connect with Carol M. Quigless at:
www.flourishwellnessoils.com
carolquiglessn.7400@gmail.com

CHAPTER 3
A Brave Heart
Marilyn Green

"Strength and Honor are her clothing: and she shall rejoice in time to come"

~Proverbs 31:25 KJV

I was married and single at the same time for many years and experiencing little to no substantial help from my ex-husband. We both struggled with being adults due to a mutuality of resentment, and we both dropped the ball in many areas. Well, you can drop a ball, but you must pick it back up when you have children and your legacy is at stake. I picked the ball back up, and he did not. I must admit that I wanted to throw the ball down, but I knew that I could have messed up a generation with the wrong decision. I must admit that I was in a state of mental paralysis and was often quite bitter and very resentful. Nevertheless, life kept moving, and I began my journey to earning my brave heart badge.

Getting through a devastating divorce, having a single source of income with no money in the bank, adolescence hormones, my own hormones, a fight for child support, working to keep the faith, and battling the storm took a lot of God - praying, fasting, repeat. I was determined to equip my sons with what they needed for the future, because I knew that they had my DNA and it was not going to be an easy road for them. I was determined that we were not losing our home, they were not leaving private schools, and they were going to college and finishing in 4 years.

We had a family meeting, and I laid out a plan to move our broken family forward. My sons' job was to study, get good grades, and graduate from high school. My job was to work (one year I had 5 – W-2s), provide for them, and manage the household. All minds were clear. My youngest son gave me an official title, "Captain". Once we knew what to ask God for by faith, I believe that we were able to sit down and allow God to stand up in our lives, and He poured all types of grace and favor. I liken it unto the journey of the Israelites - we were never hungry, and our clothes and shoes did not wear out. He was truly Jehovah Jireh, our provider. We had many unfavorable incidents to come our way during those hard years, but we were determined to complete our goals.

You may ask what happened with our lives. Well, both of my sons graduated from the same prestigious university in 4 years. One is a professor at a major university in Texas, and the other one is a senior architect for a major corporation in Georgia. Oh, I am still living in the same house. All goals were accomplished. Thank, God!!! We survived!!!

I survived and kept surviving and kept surviving. Finally, one day, God began to open my eyes to exactly what I had been through all those years. I did not automatically rejoice and say, "Thank you, Jesus." Instead, I found myself very scared and weeping. The reflections kept coming at different times and then God told me that He could not let me see what I was going through because I would have become afraid and scared and probably just give up on His inheritance – my children. I know now, while I was going through the toughest times that God hid me under the shadows of His wings and His grace was sufficient. God began a healing process on me through this whole journey, and I can say today that I am truly healed, no more resentment, no more bitterness, no more nothing about the journey. I earned my brave heart badge. God did it for me, and He is willing to do it for you and the requirements to receive the transformation that you need comes by always trusting Him and, being obedient to his Word, no matter what you might see or believe. A measure of faith is given to all and deciding to build that measure of faith by praying, praising, and pausing (to hear) are truly the keys to being victorious, God's way.

> *"If you don't go after what you want, you'll never have it. If you don't ask, the answer is always no. If you don't step forward, you're always in the same place."*
>
> **~Nora Roberts**

Marilyn Green

Marilyn Green is a native of East St. Louis, Illinois. Marilyn believes that we are all connected. And that when you win, we all win. She is the host and producer of her own podcast called, "Girl, Who Don't You Know?!" on Facebook and YouTube that allows her guests the opportunity to "transform minds, one show at a time". She is the CEO of her consulting business, JFY Consulting. She and her collaborative team assist nonprofits with grant writing, researching, and reviewing. She also teaches grant writing and has successfully taught over 300 students. She firmly believes that she can teach anyone how to manufacture a competitive grant proposal.

Working with her son, Marilyn has published a policy brief, "Appealing for an Appeal Process for Short-Term Suspension in North Carolina" for the Center for Racial Equity in Education (CREED), a nonprofit organization

Connect with Marilyn Green via email at aheartthatisbrave@gmail.com

CHAPTER 4
Becoming Light After Loss
Shontae Horton

I found out I was pregnant with my second baby girl. I remember my first few visits to this particular obstetrician. He didn't honor my request to check my blood pressure throughout my visits and I was filled with joy just like your average mama. At 11 weeks pregnant, I learned that my baby was on the smaller side. I didn't think anything of it, because I was small as a baby.

The doctor told me my baby only had one artery instead of two in the umbilical cord. Also, I was told that her heart wasn't developing well. So we had to meet with a genetic counselor to ensure she didn't have any birth defects. The doctor wanted me to get an amniocentesis, but I was only 12 weeks pregnant and the chances of her surviving that procedure was too great to risk it, so I declined. After not being heard by this provider, I decided to walk away from him and go to another obstetrician, who not only heard me but saved my life and delivered my baby breathing at 24 weeks gestational. For that, I am grateful.

I remember after each ultrasound the doctor kept telling me that my placenta was all over the place. This meant that I had Placenta Previa; it covered all of my cervix. This turned into Placenta Accreta, which means that my placenta grew too deep into my uterine wall. This led to major complications that included the loss of my daughter Naomi Shivani.

At five in the morning, I woke up thinking I had to use the bathroom. I felt this small pressure at the bottom of my stomach and then all of sudden a gush of blood came out. I remember crying my eyes out and calling her dad to let him know that I'm going to the hospital. I was so scared, not knowing what was going to come next. I went to the hospital and after being there for a few hours, they discharged me. Her heart was beating strong, and they weren't too concerned.

Before even getting up with my discharge papers, I started bleeding again. That's when it was decided that I was going to stay in the hospital until I was 30 weeks, then they would take her out. Being the optimistic person that I am, as well as trusting God. I was ready to stay in the hospital for that duration.

As a few days went by, friends and family visited me. My mom and my three-year old daughter would come and spend time with me. That was hard, not being able to be with my daughter. She was confused, and my mom was scared. It was a very uncertain situation wrapped in hope.

At 11 PM on April 26, I started bleeding. But this time, it wouldn't stop and it was heavy. The nurses ran in and placed IV's all over as they explained to me that they'll have to take her out in the morning, because I was bleeding so much and now the baby was in distress. I remember crying so hard while my grandma held my hand, and I was so scared but more scared for my baby than myself. At the time, I was unaware of how much danger I was in.

A few minutes before 6 AM on April 27, at 24 weeks gestation, my obstetrician, social worker, high-risk doctors, nurses, and neonatologist all surrounded me, telling me that they did not have tubes to fit her in the NICU once she's born, and that she would not survive. They talked about how I needed to prepare for that, that she wasn't going to survive the delivery. Also, they were going to give me a hysterectomy. Tears running down my face, all I could say was "The tubes are going to fit my baby. I know they will. We'll start with that." Guess what? The tubes fit my baby. During my procedure, I had a placental abruption, and I was cut horizontally and vertically. The first thing my obstetrician said to me was that she was able to save my uterus, and they rushed Naomi to the NICU.

One of the most overwhelming feelings was being wheeled to the NICU to see my tiny baby. Seeing her with IV's, oxygen tanks, and wires everywhere was a lot. But she was here, that's what I focused on. I remember the NICU nurse telling me I was making her suffer, that hurt me to my core because she made it seem as if, wanting my baby to live made me a horrible mom. But I just wanted her to live, I just wanted my baby girl.

May 5, 2015, after eight days, Naomi passed away in my arms, while I was surrounded by my mom and grandma. During those eight days, she received blood transfusions, multiple scans, multiple oxygen machines, and had jaundice, but she was strong. She was moving her little legs and arms and opening her eyes. She was really doing her best. On that last day was my first time holding her, I saw her heart rate go up and oxygen go up. "What if I had held her the whole time?" was all I could think." In anger, I felt I could've held her longer while she was alive, but the hospital didn't provide the support I needed. My goodbyes were cut short.

As I walked out of the hospital without my baby, I didn't understand why I had to lose her. My heart was aching, my body was in pain and I just wanted to be alone. My mom took care of my daughter, because I couldn't be what I needed for my daughter. I laid in my bed not wanting to do anything. and nobody close to me had experienced this kind of pain that I was going through. But, I am grateful I didn't have to be "strong". I was allowed to grieve. During that journey of grief, I found peace in seeking GOD. I turned to God, because I knew I couldn't heal by myself.

I remember just talking to God and playing the Kirk Franklin song, "He'll Take the Pain Away." I started to believe that I knew that GOD would take the pain away, and he did. He comforted me during one of the most challenging times in my life. I leaned on the Lord, and just like he promised, He helped me. He restored me. I will always mourn my baby girl Naomi, but finding rest in GOD led me to become the light after loss. I found rest in God through journaling, studying His Word, and meditating, even though most times it was just silence and tears. I found comfort in reading God's word daily and understanding his promises of relief from the burden of pain and grief. In the midst of my deep pain, I was lifted up by his love for me, his comfort, his support, his understanding of my confusion and desperate need for answers. Even though I can't explain why Naomi died, I am at peace when I pray to God.

Here I am today, encouraging women who've experienced this heaviness, letting them know that it's okay to react to this pain. It's okay to question God. It's okay to be jealous of other women who are carrying babies or are with their babies. It's okay to be angry and confused, but I encourage you to find a higher power that will give you peace and comfort in your heart. Once you find that peace, these feelings will subside and you will become light. You will become that person you envision, the person that can talk about their baby with a smile. The person who can tell their story with their head held high. Someone who can share the glorious promises from God that have come into fruition in life.

Take time to grieve. You need to be able to cry it out, scream it out, write it out, and talk it out. Letting it out is you taking those steps toward healing. Healing doesn't mean you will forget your baby. It doesn't mean you won't mourn your baby. It means that you're ready to live the life God has designed for you while honoring your baby. Forgive your body for not doing what it was naturally supposed to do. By forgiving your body, you can regain confidence if you're planning to try to conceive again. In addition, forgiving your body will enable you to recharge with healthy food, hydration, and hygienic habits. It starts with showing yourself love, even if you don't feel like it. A simple affirmation is "I love myself" or "I take care of my body" or "I trust my body."

Regardless of whether you miscarried, went full term and gave birth to a stillborn, or weren't given the proper medical care to detect conditions earlier, it wasn't your fault. The feeling of guilt that follows the loss of a baby is a natural reaction due to the fact that you carried the baby but did not cause the loss.

My daughter Naomi was an angel. She came here to show us what strength looks like. If this is your journey, the length of being on this earth doesn't limit the impact you can make; your baby did that for you. There's hope. There's peace. There's comfort. There's restoration, and mama, there's light.

Grief Journey Tips:

Overcoming grief looks different for everyone, but what's important to remember is that it doesn't have a timeline. You shouldn't feel rushed to grieve by your loved ones and you shouldn't judge your partner for the way he or she grieves. Our partners mourn as well but they are often forgotten about because they didn't carry the baby which causes them to mourn in silence. The best option is grace. Giving yourself grace to cry it out, be angry, be jealous, and even question GOD, because these are all natural reactions. The good part is you won't dwell in that space forever.

You can smile and laugh in the midst of grief. Grief won't always be gloomy. You may watch a funny show or find yourself getting back to your favorite hobby. Laughing and enjoying life doesn't mean you're "over" your baby. You're healing.

You will be triggered. Prepare yourself for times when you're driving past a hospital that reminds you of the traumatic experience of losing your baby there. It's okay to not want to attend baby showers and gender reveals. It's important to express to your loved one that you just can't be a part of it right now.

Ask for help. Many women suffer in silence after miscarriage, pregnancy loss, and baby loss because they are afraid of how people may view them. Sometimes, it's the hard questions about the capability of your body, if the baby had any conditions, or if you're going to try again. Seeking a therapist or grief coach or doing grief counseling does not mean something is wrong with you. It means that you acknowledge that you don't have to do this alone.

It is my prayer that you will find GOD in grief and find grace in it.

Shontae Horton

Shontae Horton is from Orange, New Jersey. She is the mother of two living children and one angel baby. Before the pandemic, she was employed as a Certified Medical Assistant. Her company, I Mother And Stuff LLC, which encourages moms to find a balance between parenting and wellness, was founded in 2020.

Since then, she has organized women empowerment workshops for single mothers. She has been featured on two virtual women's retreats and created the podcast, I Mother And Stuff, where she interviews entrepreneurs to share how they manage their busy lives. When Shontae became a Holistic Fertility Doula and an accredited life coach in 2021, she was inspired to advocate for people facing infertility.

Shontae wanted to support women and families who have experienced infant loss and encourage them to look for their purpose in the midst of their grief. In her mission, she aims to provide women and families with the mental and emotional support they deserve as a result of their experiences with infant loss.

She developed a program designed to guide and support women after infant loss called "The Light After Loss Program." Her 2022 accomplishments include completing Cornell University's Women's Entrepreneurship Program, authoring three books, volunteering and advocating for Resolve the National

Infertility Association to raise awareness about the barriers families face when trying to conceive, and earning a degree in Health Services Management from Berkeley College this coming fall.

Connect with Shontae Horton:

Website: https://imotherandstuffllc.my.canva.site/shontaehorton
IG: https://www.instagram.com/omismagriefcoach/

CHAPTER 5
I Choose Joy
Joy Green

"One of the best things you can do for this world is you become a wonderful human being. For this to happen you must take charge of your faculties. Particularly the faculties of your mind and body".

~Sadhguru Jaggi Vasudev

This chapter is about choosing to find joy in everyday life. It is about finding joy in the journey. The best thing you can do for yourself and others is to find your own happiness and live a full-fledged life. We must practice taking charge of our faculties – the powers of the mind (memory, reason, and speech). When you lose control over your faculties, you become powerless.

You Have a Choice

I know this sounds cliché, but the implications of this statement also entail the use of our free will.

When I was younger and I'd hear the term "free will", it was predominantly used in the church setting or by a religious peer. The saying "free will" was used in the sense of we have the free will to choose God or do away with religion and to choose the right thing to do instead of the wrong thing.

In the past, I'll admit, I've taken my free will for granted. Having free will isn't simply being able to choose right over wrong; it's using our free will over the struggles we face every day and choosing freedom instead of being bound by fear.

I'm learning the power of choosing joy instead of anger. For example, when my daughter locked me out of the house, and I was stuck on the patio...yep, it irritated me but only momentarily. I quickly realized it was a simple mistake and chose to laugh it off instead. Another example, choosing to follow your intuition instead of what the status quo says. Learn to trust your intuition. Yet, these are all fragmented concepts of free will - the freedom to choose being free.

I overcame severe substance abuse that took me near death. It was a choice I had to make, otherwise I was going to lose everything. It's a choice I make to this day when faced with a situation that looks like I might return to an old habit I choose not taking the self-destructive, simple way out. I make a choice about what's most important to me, my personal values and life goals.

Obstacles and Issues

Scientists estimate that genetic factors account for 40 to 60 percent of a person's vulnerability to addiction. The environment we grow up in and our behavior also play a factor in substance abuse and addiction. I have immediate family members who have battled alcohol abuse. Sometime in my 30's, I found out about a cousin who experienced severe health complications due to alcohol abuse and subsequently died from them. But that still wasn't enough to make me realize I was stuck.

Did you ever have grown up feelings at a very young age? I always felt like I wanted to be older than I was. I wanted to be an adult perhaps to escape. I felt controlled and silenced by my step-father. Trying to imagine myself as a 15-year-old drinking hard liquor is unfathomable, but that's how old I was, 14 or 15 years old. I vividly remember passing out drunk at a friend's house and I was definitely under 15 years old!

Drinking made me feel older and free. Drinking under age was also me defying the years of emotional abuse and control from my step-father. I drank to cope. I drank to not feel sad ... I drank to feel happy. Give me a reason, I was going to drink and be merry. I actually started to believe I needed to drink to be the happy version of "Joy", instead of having to feel depressed. I just didn't want to feel sad anymore.

By the age of 17 I was drinking to the point of having black-outs after a certain level of consumption of maybe six or more drinks. From the age of 17 to 29, the drinking only got worse with every life event that was thrown at me it seemed. It became easier to blame my drinking on life, so I could feel happy or just have relief from feeling emotions.

My life at 22 years old was already so draining. I was also suffering from post-traumatic stress disorder frtwo abortions, almost back-to-back at 23 years old. During my second visit to Planned Parenthood, within moments of my arrival I found myself having to get bussed off to San Francisco to complete the procedure. Someone called a bomb threat into the clinic before 9 AM! It was life-threatening, and the procedure had to be completed as soon as possible. I told practically no one what I had been through, being pregnant twice or about the bomb threat experience. Less than a year later I ended up in a hospital bed being questioned for admittance to the local psychiatric ward on a 51/50, after attempting to take my own life.

Can you blame me? I was a 23-year-old single mother with no family in the area. My bright idea was to move eighty miles away from the family and close friends I grew up with, three weeks after graduating from high school. I was running to find my independence at 18 years old with a two-year-old son. Life was a constant struggle after struggle. Drunken arguments with baby-daddy and him moving in and out of my apartment. I typically worked two to three jobs to make ends meet and provide a better life for my son.

When you've gone through so much, you feel as though you've become this angry person inside, hardened by it all. For years it felt like a cloud of doom loomed over my head; no one truly knew the pain I was in and there was no way out that I knew of. My happiness out of everyday life came from overindulging in alcohol…that was my escape. This was my vice.

I drank a lot! There were two DUI charges on my DMV record by the age of 29 years old. Those were just the times I was caught driving under the influence. I drank while driving many times. There was a point where I stopped caring about myself or life for many years. I often feel things so intensely, and humanity seems so cold…I felt out of place for most of my life. But I knew deep down inside, I was supposed to be here for something greater than just me. Unfortunately for me, it wasn't until after I gave birth to my second child that I was forced to face the fact I had a problem with alcohol abuse. At the age of 29 years old, I found myself sitting in a 55-degree jail cell.

Face the Feelings

A lot of the feelings I had surrounding my alcohol abuse were of shame and guilt…feelings of unworthiness and that something was wrong with me. The highs and lows were also a side effect of my body under constant intoxication, not allowing my organs to rest and regenerate from years of abuse.

Alcohol actually impedes the way your body absorbs fat and inhibits the absorption of vitamins A, E, and D, which normally get absorbed along with healthy fats in your diet. Vitamin A deficiency can be associated with night blindness, and Vitamin D deficiency is associated with bone softening. I realize now that the negative thought patterns I was cycling through perpetuated my overindulging in drinking and trying to numb the pain. Research has suggested that insufficient Vitamin D may compromise the immune system, and newer studies have focused on the potential link between Vitamin D and brain health. A study by the National Institute of Mental Health reinforced the notion that there may be an association between Vitamin D deficiency and a higher risk of schizophrenia (*https://www.nimh.nih.gov/health/statistics/schizophrenia*).

The nutrients I was lacking at the time played into my mental health. I felt like I was going crazy at one point … I was never going to feel happy again. Admitting to myself that my "mom wine nights" and free shots with bar patrons were now a danger to my health was extremely difficult. It wasn't fair! So many of the images on television, social media, and movies seemed to almost glorify the need for moms to wind down with wine or some other cocktail. Along my journey through rehab, I discovered my levels of drinking were not healthy or normal, even though I was embarrassed to admit it.

The Victory

It wasn't until my mid-thirties that my victory finally came, and it wasn't easy. The silver lining in this dark cloud came under the guise of another "few too many margaritas" after a late lunch Sunday meeting. Many hours after that meeting ended when I should have been home, I recall waking up from yet another black-out. Only this time I was on the phone with my mom crying and rambling on, unaware of where I was. Yet there I was, trying to "drunk-splain" to my mom who lives over 400 miles away from me, where I was at. To make the situation worse, I also drunk-dialed my boyfriend at the time to explain to him as well where I was parked. I still don't remember how I got home that night. At some point I finally sobered up enough to find my way back to the freeway and get home.

You know when you keep repeating the same bad habits in life that really cost you!?! Well, the price for my choices was everything including my life. I was caught in a cycle and still spiraling out of control from the substance abuse. I was still bartending, acting out, and making excuses for my behavior. After sleepless nights talking with my partner to convince him not to leave me, I chose to admit myself to an outpatient rehabilitation for four months. I also had to partake in community Alcoholics Anonymous meetings as a part of my recovery plan. It was the best decision I ever made! Partaking in therapy that was based around my substance abuse was something I had not faced head on. I finally made the choice to face and accept that I had a severe, lifelong problem with substance abuse, and I needed help.

Find Your Why

Suicide is the 12th leading cause of death in the United States of America. In 2020, 45,979 Americans died by suicide, and there were an estimated 1.20 million suicide attempts (*IASP. Global suicide statistics, 2021*). Death has become more common as a result of substance intake (i.e., first-time overdose) and suicide.

I overcame substance abuse and attempted suicide. I am victorious. My belief is that by shedding light on my dark times, I can show another soul who is also suffering in a similar way that it is possible to overcome and to find joy in the journey of your life. You can live your own happily ever after.

I want you to walk away feeling encouraged and empowered to take action and find ways to choose joy in your everyday life. Life can feel better.

Tips I Use to Overcome – Integrating Meditation and Mindfulness into Daily Activities and Your Lifestyle.

1. Remember, joy comes in the morning – Every day is a new day. Be intentional about every day! You can infuse joy into your day before you even get out of bed and start on your way. Take 5 minutes and play the Glad Game. Think of 10 things that bring you a feeling of joy and gladness, such as, "Listening to a baby laugh brings me joy", or "Watching my daughter enjoy the meal I've prepared for her makes me feel happy." And, "I feel grateful when I'm told I've inspired someone toward healthier choices in their life, because I shared my story."

2. Affirm this - Affirmations are positive statements that feel good. Daily affirmations are a great way to replace negative thought patterns with positive, healthy thoughts. Over many years of pain, trauma, and verbal abuse, my unconscious thoughts became the same as my experiences. Thoughts of hatred, envy, fear, jealousy, and insecurity overwhelmed my mind, and I drank because I didn't want to think about or face the thoughts in my head. Just like it took many years to instill the negative thought patterns in my mind, we must be mindful to take action to replace negative, not-so-good-feeling thoughts with words and thoughts that do feel good.

Once I dedicated time to practicing affirmations and mantras, I started to notice that I no longer felt that constant state of doom lurking over me. That terrible feeling that if something great happened, I couldn't stay happy too long or that if something great was happening, it meant that something equally devastating or worse was just around the corner. Then I finally discovered, this wasn't true at all. We operate under the Law of Attraction: a thought like unto itself attracts the same thought. Like attracts like, whether we are aware of it or not. I finally felt at peace with the thoughts I noticed passing through my mind.

3. Find your joy – Simple stress reducers: Mindful deep breathing for 3 minutes can immediately improve your mood and raise your energy level. You must take time out to discover the things in your everyday life that bring you happiness.

As the eldest daughter, I watched my mom strive to raise five amazing girls. I watched my mom be our teacher, our nurse, our best friend, our protector and joy-giver… sadly, I rarely saw my mother partake in the little things that brought her personal joy, let alone discuss with us girls about how to find that inner joy.

It wasn't until later in my adult years that I started listening to my own needs. I was oblivious to the act of radical self-care; the proclamation that you have the responsibility to take care of yourself first before attempting to take care of another. It's necessary to fill your cup first, then you can give to others from the overflow. This is what gives you the capacity to heal and to move forward into your next chapter in life.

4. Whether it's skateboarding, painting, writing music, running marathons, or even being a mentor…it's the little things in your daily life that you look forward to partaking in that add a little more joy to your own life and the lives of the souls that surround you.

5. Develop a Meditation Practice That Works for You – Mind your mind: Find ways to incorporate mindfulness practices into your daily lifestyle that bring you clarity. Meditation is a practice in which an individual uses a technique such as mindfulness, i.e., focusing the mind on a particular object, thought, or activity to train attention and awareness and achieve a mentally clear and emotionally calm, stable state of mind. Here are just a few examples of ways to include meditation in your daily lifestyle

    - Breathing Meditation – Focus your attention on your breath; the way you naturally breathe. Notice the air fill your lungs, and your chest rise as you breathe in through your nose. Feel your chest decompress, and your shoulders relax as you exhale through your mouth. Repeat this practice for at least 5 minutes two times per day.

    - Loving Kindness Meditation – Place both hands over your heart. Close your eyes and imagine someone or even a pet whom you have an immense amount of love for in front of you. As you breathe in slowly, imagine how you feel when you see this person or pet. Notice the sensation of love moving down and throughout your body, covering you with a warm feeling of joy. Slowly exhale. Repeat this practice for at least 5 minutes each day. (For best results, practice first thing in the morning)

- Walking Meditation – Connect your breathing to your steps while taking a hike or a walk. Vietnamese monk Thich Nhat Hanh made this meditation practice popular. Simply take a step with each breath. This slow walking meditation practice can be very powerful. Have fun with it - If you don't have the time or place for slow walking, just take a breath with every two or three steps while walking your dog, or in the mall while pushing the stroller or in your hallway!

Words of Encouragement

Don't you know how beautiful you are, how brightly you shine? The more often you choose your soul (the unseen), let go of the physical (seen with the eye) and the expectations, and just live, the more you become free. When you are living your truest self and can find your happiness even when life gets challenging, that's when you know you've found the key to living your happily ever after. You have the power to feel strong and choose joy even in uncertain times.

Research has shown that people perform more effectively when motivated by encouragement, reward, and self-compassion. Exercises and practices of self-acceptance and self-compassion are important parts in meditation, which may support us finding optimal ways to motivate ourselves and achieve our goals naturally. (*Tang & Tang. The Neuroscience of Mediation. United Kingdom: Academic Press Publications, 2020*).

If you are interested in learning more about finding your joy in life or working with me, you can find my books and meditation tools by connecting with me online: thejoyivefound.com.

Joy Green

Joy Green's story has been unfolding for some time now throughout the extraordinary life experiences she's had. Joy is a survivor of abuse, depression, and attempted suicide. Through meditation, yogic science, and Ayurveda, a natural system of medicine, she was able to overcome many of these deep and hidden traumas experienced from years of victimization and self-destructive behavior. Today, Joy practices as a Spiritual Coach and Transformational Speaker, successfully influencing and guiding others towards a path to better self-care, mental health awareness, and spirituality for over seven years now.

A true Libra, a lover of beauty and the arts, Joy started a career in modeling at age fifteen with the Barbizon team in San Francisco. She quickly moved on to work in television, commercials, print, and music. However, Joy's passion for the arts goes well beyond television and film. In 2015, after deciding to leave her more than twenty year career in corporate America, she began her journey as an entrepreneur and started her fashion boutique, Lace and Happiness.

Her passion for serving the community and healthy living led Joy to volunteer in the Asics half marathon raising money for "The Fulfillment Fund", which is a non-profit organization in Los Angeles working to make college a reality for students growing up in educationally and economically under-resourced communities. She continued to participate in future Asics half marathons and in

2014 decided to become a student mentor through the Fulfillment Fund program.

Giselle, an extremely shy 14-year-old 9th grader was the first student introduced to Joy. Over the years, Giselle and Joy have remained dear friends through many ups and downs including Joy's divorce, Giselle's parents' divorce, school graduations, birthdays, loss of loved ones, 12th grade Decision Day celebration, Giselle's first job, and many other life-changing events…with so many more to come.

Joy's story continues to unfold on the entrepreneurial front, being published as a co-author in the international best-seller *Your Voice Matters*. Her first published book, made it to the best-seller list in eight U.S. categories including African American History. She is in the process of writing her first edition of the book series *The Joy I've Found*, her life's story of hardship, teen pregnancy, alcohol abuse, attempted suicide, prostitution, survival, and transformation. Her story is meant to inspire others to push beyond the challenges of everyday life, find their inner voice, beauty, and joy within.

Her vivid soul is a beacon of light that allows Joy to connect with strangers and loved ones alike. Joy believes remaining open to adding her genius, love, and wisdom to every aspect of her life will ensure she reaches others in this life and beyond.

Website: https://www.thejoyivefound.com
IG: @thejoyivefound
FB: @thejoyivefound
Twitter: @thejoyivefound
LinkedIn: @joyygreen

CHAPTER 6
It Tried to Kill Me, But I Landed on My Feet!
Andrea Briscoe

Today, I am a wife, mother, grandmother, life coach, mentor, entrepreneur, motivational speaker, and community leader. Today, when you see me, you see someone who has survived and overcome obstacles. That's today…but that is not the way I started out.

Once upon a time, there was a little girl…

As a little girl growing up in Washington, DC, I dreamed of a life filled with happiness and joy. My plans included graduating from college, getting a great job, nice car, big house and meeting a cute, handsome guy; a guy who would be the man of my dreams. I dreamed of getting married and having fun in the sun. I never thought there would be any obstacles in my way to stop me from achieving my goals. After all, I was totally confident that everything would work out just as I had hoped.

As I was daydreaming about my perfect life, I started to hear and witness my parents arguing more and more. They used to be happy and joyful together. But now, they were always arguing. It felt like my whole world was falling apart. I tried not to pay attention to what they were saying, but they were so loud, I could not block out the noise; I didn't recognize them anymore. Our happy home was becoming and did become dark and gloomy. After a while, my parents sent me away to live with my grandma because they wanted to work on their marriage. When I finally returned home after three years living with grandma, it was like everything had changed. My father, who loved me and said that he would never leave me or abandon me, had left and divorced my mother. My heart was broken (into pieces) and there was a hole left in my chest where my heart used to be.

After my father left, things changed dramatically at home. My mother felt betrayed by her church friends who she trusted. She became depressed. She started drinking. She was angry all the time…not to mention, my mother was trying to provide for us with little to no money coming in. We moved so many times, that I cannot count. We were sleeping on her friends' sofas, in extra bedrooms in their homes, and in rooming houses. We finally moved to our own apartments only to eventually be evicted from the apartments and have all our stuff thrown on the curb. She would do different things just to make sure we survived.

Looking back, there was nobody to help my mother manage her feelings, the betrayal, or these situations. *Meanwhile*, my father had moved on with his life and I now felt stuck in the past and couldn't move forward. I told myself, I would not let any man walk out on me or hurt me. I would have my happy ending too! The one that I had hoped for and dreamed about.

By this time, my father had opened a church. I am a church girl at heart. My family has a long history of being involved in the church. My father, grandparents, and great-grandparents were all pastors and apostles. We've always been very spiritual and faith-oriented people which is an important part of our family's foundation. I knew from a young age that God had a special purpose for my life; even during the times that my heart was in pieces. But the pressure of being a pastor's daughter was becoming too much for me to handle. It bothered me that people thought all pastor's kids were bad because it was not true. Nobody would speak up on behalf of my sister and me; they just assumed that we were bad kids who got away with everything.

I felt isolated and alone. People loved my parents, but they didn't like or respect me enough to speak up on how we were being treated. Trying to be what others wanted me to be was not working; it wasn't who I was on the inside. Since people thought the worst of me, I decided to make sure they were right about how horrible I was by acting out and doing everything they expected of me. I remember the day I told my father I was pregnant at the age of 21 years. He said, okay, you have to apologize to the church. *Blank look – eyes blinking – eyes rolling.* This was not the response I was looking for, I wanted my father, not the pastor of the church. I wanted him to say, it's going to be okay, we will get through this. Instead, I had to stand in front of the church who did not like or care about me and apologize to the congregation who continued to whisper and drag my name through the mud, all while sitting on the back row.

This feeling of rejection from my father and the church people caused me to start partying, hang out all times of the night and drinking to numb the pain I felt inside of me; a pain that was always there, seven days a week. I was looking for love and acceptance from anybody; believing that if I could find someone who would accept me as I am, then my life would be perfect. But my quest for love led me to hang out with the wrong crowd and do things that were unhealthy and destructive.

In looking for love in all the wrong places, I met Mr. Wrong. He was a smooth talker and knew exactly what to say to a girl like me. He looked good, smelled good, was a sharp dresser and a good dancer. We looked good together and when we hit the dance floor, the crowd would cheer us on. This was what I was looking for! He would always say, "I love you", "You're so beautiful", "I cannot live without you", "I'm going to marry you", and the icing on the cake, "Baby, please don't change, you're perfect". Everything I wanted to hear and more: flowers, gifts, even wining and dining. I never spent a dime.

I started replacing friends and family with Mr. Wrong. I felt loved and protected whenever we were together. Around my family, I felt like the black sheep and sensed judgment. One day, he said that he knew a way we could make some easy and quick money. In the beginning, I did not think much about it; after all, everybody likes easy and quick money. We started doing small white-collar crimes that grew to bigger and bigger white-collar crimes. We were making so much money so fast that our lifestyle changed quickly: cars, jewelry, trips—the works! It was exciting! I had everything I wanted and more.

I did not want the money to change us or destroy our little family, so we made a pact that we would never turn our backs on each other; we'd always support each other no matter what. Those words melted my heart because I had always wanted to hear them. The money started to run out, so we had to go back to hustling, again. At first, I thought it was a one-time deal. I was not comfortable with it, but he sweet-talked me into doing it again and again. He would say things like: "You know I love you, right?; I would not let anything happen to you.; baby, I would die for you; but we have to do this, don't you love me?"

Maintaining this lifestyle came at a heavy cost and once again, I felt trapped. It looked good on the outside, but I was dying on the inside and felt rejected and alone.

My family thought I was on drugs, but in reality, I was clinging to someone who I thought was building my self-esteem. I stopped visiting my family because I knew what I was doing was wrong and illegal. I was ashamed of the way things turned out, and I didn't want to hear them say, "I knew it."

When the money ran out, he became a monster. On any given day or night, we would get into a heated verbal argument, which led us into fist fights. I knew I was in over my head, and this was not love. I tried to leave but he would remind me, "your family doesn't want you. They don't care about you, you know, I'm all you've got" and end the statement by saying, "I love you, baby. I didn't mean it." Of course, the next hour, we would be fine and then the cycle would happen all over again. One day, he got next level mad, he punched and kicked me so hard, it took the breath out of my body, and the only reason he stopped was because someone came to the door. God was watching out for me when I did not have the strength to stand. I knew this was not love because we argued and fought all the time, which reminded me of my parents before they got divorced. Every time I tried to leave; he would sweet talk me out of leaving. If you go back home, you will not have nothing and nobody. I stayed in this physical, mental, and verbal abusive relationship. There were many days that I thought about killing myself because I felt nobody loved or wanted me. I was too scared to speak up and too embarrassed to ask for help, but thank God, somebody was praying for me, and God would not allow me to take my life but gently reminded me you are not alone.

It was all fun and games, until one day we got caught, and the police arrested us. As we were on the way to jail, I remember the pact that we previously made: no snitches! But that went out the window when the police showed up. To my surprise, they named me the ringleader. I could not believe it! I thought we were a family!

Sitting in a dark jail cell with no window, no light, feeling ashamed, abandoned, and embarrassed of myself, I had put my trust in the wrong person, and now I was paying the price. What had I done? God was trying to get my attention, because he knew that I was going down the wrong path in life. I began to cry out to him, asking him to forgive me, and give me another chance. I promised that if he delivered me from this situation, I would serve him with all my heart.

Now I am released from jail, and Mr. Wrong is gone. All our stuff is gone. I'm 800 miles away from home in a city where I don't know anybody. I call home and my father gives me money for one night in the hotel and told me to go to the shelter for help. Of course, I'm crushed, and feeling rejected all over again and confirming what Mr. Wrong said: nobody loves or wants me. At that moment, I didn't know God had a plan and was orchestrating my steps to let me know that he was with me and that he loved me.

So, I stayed in the hotel for that night then became homeless; I had no money. I refused to call home again and didn't want to ask my mother because she was taking care of my daughter. I slept at the airport, bus stations, outside on park benches, under bridges, or anywhere I could find a safe place where I could get food and water out of the trash or on café tables.

This was a new low point in my life. I remembered the words from my father and I went to the shelter. I got tired of sleeping on the streets trying to figure out what was next. Back home, I had a house with warm beds and food in the refrigerator and now I was living in a shelter and stranded from everyone that mattered to me.

Living at the shelter was a big adjustment. There was a cot for each resident to sleep on, but we had to watch our belongings, because people would steal from you if you weren't careful. I was assigned a case manager, Ms. Alice, who kept reminding me that this situation would not last forever; God would restore.

All the people at the shelter looked forward to Sundays because the church vans would come and pick them up and take them to church. The church also provided food for the residents, and all they had to do was attend services. At first, I was not going because I was still trying to do it on my own, but the other residents kept talking about how great it was there and how much better they felt after attending services. Three weeks later, I decided to try it out myself. At first, it was uncomfortable because I did not feel like I belonged, but at the end of the service, an elderly lady hugged me and said, "GOD LOVES YOU." This happened three weeks in a row by three different people. The next week, I felt a calmness over me like I'd never felt before and knew that I would be able to get through this situation.

I was ready to go to church the next Sunday, looking for the elderly ladies to let them know how much they helped me. But I couldn't find them. We sat through service, and another lady came up and said, "GOD LOVES YOU." I began pouring my heart out to her, from start to finish. She listened patiently and prayed with me, calling me later in the week just to check on me and remind me that I was loved and not alone.

As I got settled into my new job as an office manager, I was also trying to get my first legal apartment (in my name only) and preparing to be a mother to my daughter. The police showed up at my job and arrested me again in front of everybody in the office, but it was different this time… This time, God was with me.

Now, I'm back in jail standing before the judge and received a 25-year sentence, but I knew this prison cell would not be my final destination. I kept telling myself, "I'm coming out." The last time my father visited me in prison. He reminded me of what God's word says, and to pray for the answer and not the problem. I requested for my sentence to be reviewed; the courts scheduled a court date. When I got the new date for court, I heard God say, "You're coming out." I told everybody I was not coming back because God said it. I got to court and after reviewing my case, the judge said, "Time served – you are free to go home"!

What was designed to destroy me, to cause me to lose my mind, God turned it around and used it to bear witness that HE is a miracle worker. It wasn't easy but I had to experience this journey towards victory and finding "ME".

You Are Not Alone

The fear of rejection and, of being alone started when I was a child, when my parents got divorced. I knew why my parents divorced. I knew I was not the reason, but I still felt rejection, abandoned, and alone. If my dad, who I knew loved me without a doubt, could leave me, then what would stop another man from doing the same thing. I started trading in peace for chaos, going from functional relationships to dysfunctional relationships. I was selling my soul just so I would not be alone. This toxic relationship was the lowest point of my entire life, because at the end of the day, what I feared the most had happened: I was now living with Mr. Wrong, but I was alone and empty. Things had gotten so bad, I wanted to just end it all and die. I was embarrassed by my choices and lifestyle. I allowed my thoughts and fears to take over my life.

Sitting in my prison cell, I remember the bible verses from Sunday School, "Lo, I am with you always, even unto the end of the world", Matthew 28:20. God is with you at the break of day, Psalm 46:5. I fought myself, saying these words over and over and over again.

I got to the point in my life where I refused to believe the lie. I stopped believing the crazy story I kept telling myself. I refuse to participate in another sad love song. I chose to take my life back, my mind back, and my voice back.

When you get tired and fed up, it will cause you to change your scene and start singing a new song. It all starts with changing your mindset and speaking positively. When you speak, your words are feeding your mind which turns into how you see things, how you feel about something, and how you will respond to something.

"You have the power to change. Turn the table, use your power to overcome and live".

Use Your Voice

Before this toxic relationship, the old "ME" would speak her mind and say exactly what was on it but now after being mental, verbally, and physically abused, I had no voice, no words to speak. I was constantly doubting myself. My inner saboteur would remind me that nothing will ever change. There's no point, nobody wants you, nobody wants to hear you, see you, or even be bothered with you but him, Mr. Wrong, my abuser, which caused me to feel helpless and abandoned.

I remember it, like it was yesterday, after attending church, I was reminded that I have the power to change the outcome. I kept saying, I have the power to change the outcome. I am not a victim anymore. I kept saying as I walked to the bus stop and to work. I wrote it on pieces of paper and placed it at my desk, on the refrigerator, and on the mirrors in the bathroom. The more I said it, the stronger I became, and I started believing I had the power to change the outcome. I'm worth more. I desire more.

I challenge you to combat every negative thought, words, and pictures with positive reinforcement. We all know what better is; We know what better feels like; You must push past all the negative energy to get to the positive. See yourself as God sees you. God sees you beautiful, powerful, strong, and brave. Build your self-confidence by making a list of positive words and actions. Write them down, say it out loud, and believe what you're saying, "You Have the Power to Change the Outcome".

When you believe in who you are and what you want, you do not settle for people who do not also want those things for you. Finding the power to stand up is the key to finding your voice.

Reach Out & Ask for Help

It's so important to reach out and ask for help, especially when you are struggling. I know this from first-hand experience. One of the biggest mistakes I made was assuming that everybody knew what was going on in my life. I thought all my friends could read my mind and see that I was struggling. But really, they were looking at all the superficial stuff, the outer version of me - the cars, trips, clothes, jewelry, shoes - instead of looking at what was really going on inside.

I did not look like I was being abused, because I appeared to be fine. During those dark days, I was crying on the inside for help, but no one noticed. The weight of my situation became too heavy, and so I decided to ask God for help. This was a major turning point in my life, and my situation changed. God sent me friends, family, and mentors who saw my heart. They uplifted me; they pushed me to be better. It took me a long time to realize this but asking for help is not a failure. It is an admission that you cannot do everything alone. I needed God's power to make a change.

Let's start today by telling ourselves the whole truth. You are much stronger than you think. You have the power to change anything in your life. You can achieve anything you want. Walk in confidence, knowing that your legacy is victorious.

Andrea Briscoe

Homeless, jobless, shamed, and hopeless in the midst of personal adversities, Andrea Briscoe has learned how to live unstuck and is committed to helping others in their journey to freedom.

As the Founder & CEO of the non-profit organization Love You Back to Life, Andrea Briscoe is an advocate for the overlooked and those most in need; purposefully assisting them in overcoming challenges and finding their path. Her faith, her own experience overcoming homelessness and being a single mother sparks her passion to ensure every woman has the resources necessary to overcome feelings of abandonment, rejection, and loneliness.

Andrea Briscoe is an anointed evangelist, motivational speaker, and life coach with the message of empowerment to enhance one's internal core qualities to improve any situation. Additionally, Andrea is sought after to participate in many church events and conferences, all while maintaining her focus on providing the tools necessary to transform a person by getting them to recognize their own strength and self-worth.

Ongoing is Andrea's vision to help the less fortunate, which is the heart and soul of her thirty years in community outreach.

Andrea Briscoe was born and raised in Washington, DC. She obtained her Master of Arts in Religion - Evangelism and an undergraduate degree in Biblical Studies from H.E. Wood Bible Institute & Theological Seminary. She is also educated in Christian counseling, Christian leadership, youth ministry and is an experienced trainer. She is a charter member of Toastmasters International, where she mentors new members and clubs and currently serves as President of Owings Mills Community Toastmasters Club.

"Today Is The Best Day Of My Life – I have everything I need to survive"

~Andrea B.

Facebook: www.facebook.com/AndreaB.Briscoe/
Instagram: www.instagram.com/AndreaB.Briscoe/
LinkedIn: www.linkedin.com/in/andrea-briscoe/

CHAPTER 7
Not Built To Break
Lynnecia S. Eley

Often, we may think that most opposition comes from those around us like a complaining spouse, that road-raging driver on our morning commute, or an over-controlling boss, but rarely do we acknowledge the truth that we are mostly our own worst critic. Getting stuck in a cycle of self-defeating behavior is easy and getting unglued requires work – inner work, starting with yourself and coupled with **faith, courage** and **determination**.

Last year between May 7 to May 19, I was stuck feeling self-defeated, broken, and ashamed. What happened to the confident, always smiling, best friend, and motivational cheerleader that everyone knew and loved? I was lost… I was stuck.

A routine hysterectomy procedure and planned two-day hospital stay for recovery turned into multiple surgeries, 24 hours on a ventilator, 17 bags of 1000 mL fluids, 11 units of blood (enough to replace an average-sized person's entire body), countless pricks, needles, tests, and scans to keep me on the side of the living — but my fight didn't end there. I was brought back, in a partial state at first, I felt. I used the phrase "brought back" because even after more than a year later, there is still a span of about 72 hours where my memory is empty or vague; I feel like I left.

Physically being rebuilt also funneled in a need for mental repair. My spirit was broken. My drive was missing, and my passions were forced into hiding. I was recovering from a fight to live. I almost died and as I reflect on the 12 days I spent in the hospital, 8 of which were time spent in the Intensive Care Unit (ICU), I can truly relate to Whitney Houston's song "I didn't know my own strength."

Alone in a room, attached to monitors, hearing the code blue of others in the ICU unit, and without the will to move out of the bed, I found myself thinking of who was coming to usher me to my Heavenly Father. Leaning on my Christian faith and relying on Jesus's promise of *"I am going there to prepare a place for you. And if I go and prepare a place for you, I will come back and take you to be with me so that you also may be where I am"* in the book of John, I was in the waiting room, sort of speaking. I stared out the only window in the room to a tree that was wavering in the wind thinking and wondering, "Will it be my great-grandmother Ludella "Granny" or maybe one of my grandfathers?" I remember laughing out loud envisioning my grandfather James, affectionately known as "Bubba", entering the room and saying, "What's this on your head girl? Curly hair? That's not your hair, that ain't nothing but an ultra-perm", and we both laugh. Mentally I was checking out.

Days 4 and 5 were rough. Learning that I had been on a ventilator, tried to remove it myself, and not have any memory of the prior days, I was met with the biggest challenge I didn't see coming. On day 4 I was assigned a night nurse that at first sight reminded me of my grandmother. At 7 PM, her smile was kind and her introduction was gentle. At 2 AM she was someone else. On a usual night, I'm a light sleeper, but being away from home, monitors beeping, and in constant pain, I didn't do any sleeping and my night nurse was not having any of it. I can see her frustration growing each time I called for help to the restroom or to drop the air because I was steaming from night sweats. On one occasion she stormed into the room in response to my call saying "YOU NEED TO GO TO SLEEP! I'm going to give you something, so you can stop calling me every few minutes." That she did and for the next 24 hours I was a potato. I recall my physical therapy nurse coming to my bedside saying, "Let's go for a walk" and through drowsy eyes, barely parting my lips, I said, "I can't move". I also remember opening my eyes and seeing my husband sitting in the room and having just enough strength to say "babe" before falling back asleep. A few hours later, I learned that Rose, the night nurse, had given me a cocktail of medicine that included morphine, fentanyl and Benadryl. My God, she was trying to take me out. That night Rose was assigned to me again. I admittedly kicked her out of my room and prayed the entire night NOT to need her, and I didn't. Neither did she step foot in my room that night except to check vitals and we never spoke any words to each other.

Day 6 of being in the ICU was pivotal. As I laid in the hospital bed, I was drawn to commotion outside my room door. A team of doctors were meeting and conducting their rounds. I did not notice my physician there, so I wasn't paying much attention, just being nosey to the chatter. Until one doctor peered into my room and directly into my eyes and asked with a finger pointing, "What's going on in here?" Another doctor flipped a few pages and started rattling off data. I didn't hear much of the stats, because I was locked in eye contact with this doctor who also seemingly wasn't listening as well. He walked into my room and said, "Young lady, how are you doing?" Already defeated, I responded with a shrug… no words, just a weakened shrug of the shoulders and dropped my head.

In the room walked the other doctors and I can hear one reporting, "She's been here since Friday after a total hysterectomy plus unilateral salpingo-oophorectomy", which means everything was removed except one ovary. He continued on saying, "She was diagnosed with Disseminated Intravascular Coagulation (DIC) and small bowel obstruction." Prior to this day, doctors had a tube that went from my nose, down my throat, and into the top of my stomach that pumped out waste and gas, since I was unable to move my bowels naturally. The Nigerian doctor began asking questions about options that we had already tried, medications that weren't working in the immediate time frame, when he looked at me and said, "You can't go?" I shrugged again and nonchalantly said no. He stared for a brief second and then turned to the nurse and said "Find me some chewing gum", then kicked everyone out the room and closed the door.

He looked at me and said with the most sincerity in his voice and vision, "You have to get up. You cannot sit here and act beaten down. You are not broken. Get up!" In this moment I felt these words in my soul. I started to cry, tears that confirmed what he saw in me. Tears that woke up my faith. Acts 12:7 says, *"And, behold, the angel of the Lord came upon him, and a light shined in the prison: and he smote Peter on the side, and raised him up, saying, Arise up quickly. And his chains fell off from his hands."* Dr. Adekunle was my angel, sent with a special message that loosened the chains of defeat and pulled me out of the "waiting room". When the nurse returned with chewing gum, he said chew this as the motion of chewing activates the muscles of the bowels and will help you begin to go. And as I chewed the first stick, he danced all over that ICU room saying, "Get up and move. Don't just sit there. Chew and move. Trust me, it will help." … And it did, so much more than he knows.

On day 7, still chewing gum, I had my first sign of relief and renewed faith that I was soon to be going home, and I was determined to get that tube out of my nose. I choked, coughed up blood and mucus, the nurse ran in and said that she was rushing me to another CT Scan and possible surgery. I kicked and screamed and asked for my phone. I called my husband crying and told him to call my surgeon and have her help me get out of ICU, and he did. Minutes later I got a call from Dr. Paccione, and she asked why I was still there and demanded to talk to whomever was in charge that shift. Things started to happen around me, and all the nurses were giving me dirty looks. That's when I knew my doctor read them their rights. By nightfall, one of my original nurses walked in and said, "I remember you. I spoke to your husband on surgery day, when you were in an induced coma after bleeding out. Why are you still here, what's wrong?" I recanted my last few days and ended with "I just want this tube out", and he said "Well, let's take it out then". In a matter of moments, I was freed, and within a day, I was transported out of ICU and into a regular hospital room. I was out of critical care, but my fight was not over.

Happy to be out of ICU, I greeted the first physician to check on me with a full smile but was weak and barely able to lift my own arms to wave hello. She looked at me and said you must eat and rebuild your strength; you're going home soon. I immediately thought again to my foundation of faith, where in 1 Kings 19:7, it says, *"And the angel of the Lord came again the second time, and touched him, and said, Arise and eat; because the journey is too great for thee."* How can I give up now? I thought... the Confidence Doula herself, the author of Birth with Purpose, the coach that teaches others to pursue their passions at all cost and birth the purpose that God has given them – where is she?

In that moment, the woman that many others looked up to, the woman that has coached other women and young teens to be filled with self-awareness, confidence, and courage was stuck. Coming from a line of resilient women, I was not taught to give up. There's always a way, and nothing or no one can hold me back. Yet, there I was - stuck and afraid... because I'm human. My first instinct when confronted with an emotionally draining challenge is to run. As much strength as I have because of my faith, I still struggle with feeling like a victim and fighting my own nervousness and anxiety to do things that push me out of my comfort zone. We are all imperfect beings, but must thank God for His grace and peace that surpasses all comprehension.

Fear is that one thing that can hold us back, and taking action to overcome fear can boost your confidence and provide motivation and resilience. I had to reaffirm myself and my passions and reasons to live. Be still and listen like Psalm 27:14 teaches us to *"Wait for the Lord; be strong, and let your heart take courage."* Courage is the conduit to confidence and the enemy of fear. Confidence comes from believing we can do something; courage is giving it a go – the green light, despite our fears. I replaced fear with faith by surrendering to God. I then added courage and moved forward to determination.

Throughout this experience, I've learned that I am unbreakable. I am victorious, and I got to TRULY know my own strength. There are many definitions of the word "strength". Similar to resilience and fortitude, I'm referring to strength as defined by the Oxford Languages Dictionary as "the emotional and mental qualities that are necessary in dealing with situations or events that are distressing or difficult". These 8 strength qualities below helped me overcome and pick myself back up.

Support, **T**rust, **R**esilience, **E**ndowment, **N**ecessity, **G**race, **T**enacity, and **H**appiness - **STRENGTH**

A gift, a talent, an asset — ME! God provisioned value and gifted me with love and many passions — dare I give up on my purpose?

Life testimonies are often built from unplanned and/or uncontrolled experiences that in some ways were necessary. Necessary to break through a roadblock or to provide courage to someone else who thought they'd never make it through. My experience was necessary to honor and trust the support system I have around me, reprogram my default to doubt myself, and to finally acknowledge that tomorrow's happiness begins today by going on a journey of being whole on your own because you are already qualified. Not qualified in terms of accolades and credentials, but qualified in terms of your calling, your passions, and your purpose.

My experience is not singular. I was in a state of distress and needed refuge. There are many women who suffer in silence with fibroids or other medical conditions, and we do so because we've been conditioned to deal with our circumstances or pretend that they don't have any direct effects on us. Most times it's our mental capacity and well-being that needs more care and grace. I thank

God daily for being my pillar of faith, courage, and determination. Knowing that He sent his angels to surround and uplift me deserves all my praise.

I got to know my own strength, because I was not built to break. And guess what, neither are you – Stuck Is NOT Your Story!

Lynnecia S. Eley

Lynnecia S. Eley is a career-driven entrepreneur, wife, and mother. Born and raised in Miami, Florida, she is an award-winning University Assistant Dean and Adjunct Professor that is committed to excellence, dedication, and caring for others. Known as the Confidence Doula, Lynnecia is an author and coach providing guidance and support to help women and young adults feel self-assured in their abilities to ***Birth with Purpose***.

Through content, training, and workshops, she guides others to truly identify with the conception of their ideas and understand that they are already purposeful. As an adjunct professor, she fosters rigorous and inclusive conversation in the classroom that explores personal values and relationships to test the character and responses of people when faced with ethical dilemmas.

Lynnecia is also the co-founder of Two Queens Media, Soigne' + Swank Magazine® and HER Professional Society - all brands that promote and support community growth in business, education, and the media/publishing space. She is a Certified DISC Personality Analyst and Business Coach. She received her bachelor's in business management from the University of Phoenix in 2009, earned her executive master's in program and portfolio management from Georgetown University in 2018, and holds many professional and graduate certificates.

Connect with Lynnecia S. Eley:
Website: www.shecaninspire.com
Facebook: www.facebook.com/shecaninspire2
Instagram: www.instagram.com/shecaninspire

CHAPTER 8
Army Strong Built Ford Tough
Tracey Ford

Dancer, cleaner, cook, people pleaser, and motormouth – all these just about sum up Tracey Lynn Ford, born in Louisiana and raised as a Creole girl. I always wanted to make people happy. I loved looking at happy people. When people are happy, it makes me feel good. I loved doing things for people to make them smile.

From grade school to high school, I loved music and art. Both are uniquely designed but are almost the same. I love seeing people use the gifts God blessed them with. It's not a secret that dancing is my gift, which also makes people happy. But making people happy was not very good for me all the time. It could be overwhelming, too. Sometimes, when I'm unable to do something for somebody, they tend to forget all the things I did for them. You could say I had a problem saying no, that I can't help explaining myself.

Everywhere I go, people would ask me to dance or show them how to. Music is therapeutic. It can heal one's pain, take you to both happy and peaceful places. Baby! Music has been my pain-reliever for years. Since dancing has been my lifesaver, I never shied away from sharing my love for it to other people. Dancing has brought me and others unity and love. Throughout my career, I have included dancing in everything I do, and I truly believe it has saved so many people.

Let me share with you how I overcame death. How I disappointed the devil. How Stuck could never be my story. Every L in our life is not a loss. It's sometimes a lesson. My deployment was the most honorable & traumatic experience in my life. I was down and out. Even doctors told me I was just not going to be normal again. But God has a way of showing you He is God. It is important to never give up on yourself even on your last breath. We must always fight until the end. One thing I will always keep with me from my upbringing is my granny raised us to pray and fight until the end. I was raised on W 28th Ave in Covington, La. One thing about back then everyone was family or everyone knew your family. So our mindsets were different from the kids today. I tried to remember those days right when my life changed unexpectedly. In January 2003, I was mobilized to deploy to Iraq. I was an army soldier waiting to go serve in War. I underwent many weeks of training, and I was so motivated. I was an M249 SAW gunner, so I was considered to be "high-speed low drag". To be a female soldier and have a squad automatic weapon speaks volumes.

I became a part of the 1498th Transportation Company. Although my actual unit was the 40th ID Infantry Brigade. However, for mobilization, soldiers are taken from different units and combined based on their actual military occupational specialty. Your job is to do whatever you are good at, and I thought I was good at several things back then. You know when you're feeling like Rambo or Rocky. G.I. Jane. Long story short, we were called to duty to support Operation Iraqi Freedom & Operation Enduring Freedom.

Families were saying their last goodbyes, but also there were people getting sent back upon failing the mobilization process. In numerous briefs, I can still hear my First Sergeant saying what the mission was and how serious it was and what we were going to do so that we can all come back home safe to our loved ones. This was the first time I felt I could really do something and make a difference in the world. After all, September 11th really changed my life forever. I was just ready to get over there and do what we needed to do. I was a good 110 pounds soaking wet. A fitness guru. I loved dancing and running. I was very afraid, but I would never show it. I was walking around with that heavy rucksack and my weapon.

Once we arrived in Iraq with our boots on the ground, it wasn't what we thought it would be. It was just sand and dirt with tents everywhere and heat that was indescribable. Lord, have mercy, child. But we were still ready. From the platoon leaders to 1SG and all the way up the chain of command, we were unprepared for what was to come. I have to say it was very disorganized, but we were just ready to go to war. We had handheld radios that only worked from one beacon light to the next beacon light on a vehicle. I drove a heavily equipped tactical tractor, which is an 18-wheeler in the civilian world but more sophisticated and technical to say the least. We had very little ammunition, a few uniforms, and maybe two pairs of boots. But we still had high speed soldiers that came to do a job for our country.

We made our own metal to put on truck doors. We made our own communication for the trucks. We borrowed trucks from different units to complete missions. We hauled porter potties or toilets, tanks, trucks, and lockers. You name it, we loaded and unloaded it. We would even fuel in Scania on the side of the road. We didn't even have chow halls (dining facilities) set up then at that time.

There were many nights when I didn't think we would make it from one destination to another. The dirt was like snow asphalt. You could never see what was in front of you until it was too late, so the convoys were very dangerous. Most of the troops were so young and inexperienced throughout our deployment. I was attached to many other active-duty units. A couple of times we lost within the convoys. The convoys would mount up and leave, not knowing they left some of their own soldiers behind. The only thing you can do is wait for them to realize they left you and pray you meet up with your actual Unit on the road. In between convoys you just read letters or write to loved ones. Sometimes, it would be weeks before you could connect back to your actual unit.

I didn't have anyone really when I was deployed. My family wasn't the type to check on me or actually worry about me. I truly felt this way all my life, but my family has always been my priority. I always wanted to do better for myself and for my family to make them proud. My goal since I was a young girl was to give my Mom the world. Then it became a priority when she became sick. I have always wanted to provide better for my children. My siblings were doing their own thing. Mommy was still off and on sick but she was still doing ok. My Aunts were helping my Mom. They basically took their Life and revolved it around helping care for my mother. This was something my family often did. We care for our elderly sick and raise each other's children. My sister & younger brother were still really young when I left for the military. The younger ones were trying to still find their way in life. One of my brothers moved with me to San Diego, CA to take care of things while I was deployed. I wanted to show him a better life as well. My other brother was actually married and he had 2 kids at the time and he actually was in another household, we only shared the same dad but he was always and still loving and supportive. I kind of always wanted to be the one they all looked up to. I am the oldest but they all loved my brother Goldy. I say that he was the favorite. My mom was always a sweetheart but she can turn into a firecracker. I loved my father but didn't like him very much. There were many things I didn't understand as a child that I was left to figure out. My father was very strict on me. I blamed my parents for not allowing me to be a kid. I always had to be like a grown up. When I was at War, I didn't really have anyone that was in my immediate family. They didn't come to my graduation from Basic Training. My Mom did whatever my Dad said to do. She was very submissive. I truly needed my Mom so much when I was deployed. I needed family and friends. I begin to finally accept that I was angry all these years because of my relationship with my family. Mainly, my father. Needless to say, once I thought I was going to die in Iraq at one point because things were so bad, I wrote my father a letter telling him he was horrible & his mental abusive ways sometimes affected my ability to function as an adult. I was also angry at my mom for allowing him to discipline us the way that he did when we were kids. I told him everything I held back for years. I was very hurt, I care for my father and I just did not agree with his method of raising children. So I told him how his actions caused me to make decisions in my life that weren't always the best. Well after coming off of a Convoy a month later, and I was still alive for the mail call. I was very shocked when I received his letter. I thought if I didn't die in Iraq, that my father would come to kill me after everything I told him in my letter. I was never going to take it back because he needed to hear it. I never expected that he would apologize but I know that there is a God, and he is a loving and forgiving God. My dad's letter was a sincere apology. He agreed that he was not a good dad. He said he was also hurt as a kid. He told me things I never knew. I remember what he did to us, how he treated us, and the hurt. Throughout my counseling I realized that hurt people hurt people, so his apology meant everything, especially when he owned up what he did. I was able to move forward with my life. I felt the heavy load of hurt and anger was taken off my shoulder. I was able to start healing and it helped me become a better person as well. I honestly believe that our childhood experiences affect us in our adulthood.

I want to mention my cousin Shirley Y, who was like my angel when I was in Iraq. She wrote to me and sent me cookies and packages, which gave me comfort and hope. My cousin Ronald B. would ask my family about me. I don't think I would have gotten through a lot of the stressful times in Iraq without Shirley support. I would ask people about Abita and Covington how everything was going. One thing I know about My Cities, They go hard and pull through in spite of trouble or hardship. I was grateful my kids were doing great with their grandparents and Tia was so intelligent, outgoing, and spoke Spanish. Treavor didn't care for school as much but he loved to play music and he thought he was a DJ. My kids were in separate homes & states. NOLA was always full of surprises but my son was always ok. The phone calls back home always gave me hope that I would make it back, but after they hung up, stress sets in. I would try to focus on everything but home to get through most days. Without me playing music or doing dance routines to make people try to forget where we were. They would say we were going home but then something else would come up. So many of us were getting split up and sent to other units. Everywhere I went, everyone knew me. I was either Lil 504 or Goldy.

I always tried to make things upbeat. The soldiers were getting relaxed, and it was a blessing because we were all tense. In each formation we would get bad news or information from another convoy. Again, the convoys continued to make mistakes leaving troops behind. The last time my unit left us, we got hit. life after that went downhill for me. I ended up getting medevaced to Landstuhl, Germany. I didn't know then but I know now. The truck in front of us ran over an IED improvised explosive device, which caused shrapnel to explode everywhere with some going into my breast, different parts of my body, and my bladder. The jump caused trauma to my bladder, which permanently disabled me. They said I would have complications and probably would get my bladder removed that year. I was warned about bladder and kidney cancer due to shrapnel that had entered my body. The doctor could not determine if the bladder could be saved but the blow to my pelvis was so bad that bone fractures pierced my bladder wall causing me to have all types of urethral disorders. Later on, I was diagnosed with interstitial cystitis. There's no cure for interstitial cystitis. There was no way of knowing if the full bladder or the jump caused more damage, and I was told so many different things. I had shrapnel in my arms and breasts. My right jaw bone was dislocated, and my teeth were chipped. I experienced head trauma and other minor injuries with my knees and right toe but the worst was the injury to my bladder.

They said I had to get out of the Army now, because I would never have a normal life again. My bladder, they thought, would never work again. They even told me I would never use my colon as I normally used to because it was also affected. I was out of it for almost three days before I even knew where I was or what had happened to me. After my commander from the 40th ID Infantry Brigade found out that I was awake, he told me about my diagnosis and about Hurricane Katrina. You see, while I was going through war and fighting for my life, my family in Louisiana was hit by Hurricane Katrina. We were going through a tragedy on both ends and didn't know it. Well, my chain of command went to Louisiana and found my mom and her sisters at a hotel. They brought them ready-to-eat meals and water. Hurricane Katrina had destroyed Louisiana. New Orleans was horrific. Katrina was a disaster. Louisiana people truly are Soldiers. They fight wars daily.

After recovering enough to get transferred back to the States, I went home to absolutely nothing. My kids were living with different grandparents, and the things I used to have, I no longer owned. The relationship I was in was over. They had to sell my stuff and keep the things they wanted, while the rest was thrown away. I had to start all over again from scratch while going through medical procedures and the Army saying then that they needed to get me boarded and see if they could still keep me on active duty orders. Now I am facing being discharged. I was put on so many medications. I underwent seventeen bladder procedures and three bladder surgeries. I didn't recognize myself anymore. My Captain told me that the medical board was evaluating my disability along with my profile. Then the heartbreaking news. I was told I would be medically discharged from the U.S. Army. I felt like I had jumped from the tactical tractor all over again. I felt like going to sleep & never waking up.

I was depressed because all I knew was being in the Army. I came back from the war hurt and broken with my family also having just suffered devastation from a hurricane, and the Army was saying they could not keep me because I can't play anymore for them. I went through so many emotions at that time. People that used to look up to me were then looking down on me. My kids were angry because I missed too many important events in their lives like graduations, dances, and proms. Just wasn't there as a Mom. I let them down. I felt I was a failure I was hurting, and I was handicapped. I was not the same when I first left for deployment.

The military said they were my family. I need my Family. I looked for the military to have my back, but nobody seemed to care when I was broken. My unit did not even contact me. I had to walk around with a catheter in BDU Uniform. Then I wore PT gear with adult diapers. I was mentally drained, in pain, and embarrassed. I served my Country. Many were not there for support but some people remained in my family - Master Sergeant Adam Henson. SSG Billups also was there for me and my daughter for so much. I actually was adopted later on by the Twisted Motorcycle Club that became my actual family from 2008 until present. My sister Spicy actually shared her mom with me, Mama Majoni may she rest in peace, God knew I needed a family being I was so far away from home. Twisted is my family for life. My Army MSG Post still checks on me and a few others.

Because of the U.S. Code Orders from the President to the Armed Forces defining our job, Title 10 and Title 32 Orders, I had to fight for my benefits. I was so weak and on so many medications that I was not in my right mind. I had a friend from home who was like a best friend and whom I had dated before my military career. Travis later left Bogalusa, La to come to San Diego, Ca. He helped me when I had all those tubes everywhere and although he did not know what he was facing, he never ever gave up. He never became afraid and never ran away. He is still one of my best friends regardless of any situation and if I need him I know he will be there and vice versa. Medically I was suffering from Post-Traumatic Stress Disorder and seizures. I didn't have any family to help nurse me to health. My mom had a stroke, while my kids were in their junior high grade school years. I just did not know what was going to happen next. All I did was pray. I knew God would never bring me this far only to leave me. I literally went to war for my country. I had made a better life for my kids and earned a better education. Yet, here I was suffering, and I felt that that was it for me. But I kept praying to God. In John 14:6 Jesus said, "I am the Way, the Truth, and the Life. No man cometh unto the Father but through Me." So there was no way that God would have led me here only to drop me off. But I felt lost. My son had a child, my first grandchild but I was not in a good relationship with my son. I was not at my best, I was mentally messed up so I could not have a relationship with my grandchild. My kids were hurt. I was lost and mad, not realizing they were going through hurt while I was hurting. Tia my mini me, she is the Hero, a little girl that had to grow up from Louisiana to Puerto Rico to California & Mommy in and out of her life. Still she graduated college and excels in everything she does. My son owns his own business as well as a supervisor. Then I looked at myself and I failed them. I was Miss High Speed, and I was going to make a difference in the world. And yet, my world was falling down on me. My comrades had died, I became injured in the war, and permanently disabled as well but I did what was right, putting my life on the line to protect my country. People who have no idea what I have been though keep calling me a hero. I was not sure what I was and I thought that a hero was far from it but, I played the part even though I was crying constantly.

I am not a hero. My kids were the heroes. I was mentally gone. I could not even go to a store without standing sideways because I could not allow anyone to stand behind me. I slept in a closet. I had nobody to help me get through. Where was everyone? I was in a wheelchair. I had to catheterize myself. I don't think anyone would fully understand all this, especially if it is something you are never used to. I have been medically boarded, waiting to be released, and the other high-speed soldiers kept looking at me like I'm a handicap case. The whole time I wished I was either still fighting in the war or I was dead with my comrades.

Every time I used the bathroom, it felt like a razor blade was cutting me. They were not sure if I was passing foreign body objects or kidney stones. Try to be me for a second. This happens every time you urinate. You would be screaming and crying. You won't even feel when it's coming, and when you do, it is too late. You're not only in pain constantly, but also embarrassed and going through all of it alone. Everyone has given up on you. I was 110 lbs. give or take when I was going into war. Since the injury and the steroids, I weighed 231 lbs., wearing an adult diaper and going through bladder therapy daily.

I was constantly reminded that my disability is permanent and there is no cure for it. I was away from home, trying to figure out my next plan because this was my future. I served in the military, and I wanted to give back to the community. But how am I supposed to have a plan when I am on all types of medications and appointments every day. One minute, I would be talking then the next minute, I would be crying then laughing. I let the doctors count me out. They keep saying I would never walk right or even dance again. Running was out of the question. I absolutely gave up on myself without keeping my faith in God. You see, I came home to nothing. My health. My career. My family. All of these were gone. The home I used to have had been sold because the person I was with before I went to war never returned to the old house. The court ordered the tenants out. I was deployed at that time, not knowing any of it. I just hit rock bottom. I had never felt so low.

Philippians 4:13 says, "I can do all things through Christ who strengthens me." And God came through. He gave me strength to keep going. Enough strength that I am alive to see Him replace the apartment with a two-story home and brand-new furniture. I have a top-of-the-line medical bed where I can be comfortable even after my surgeries and procedures. I was also given the opportunity to be nominated to do the Heroes at Home television show.

The bladder they said I would never use on my own I am still using up to this day seventeen years later. I have not had my bladder removed, and I was not diagnosed with bladder cancer. I took myself slowly off the medication and started trying to walk daily. I am back dancing and teaching fitness and health classes all over the world, sharing my testimonies to help others with interstitial cystitis disease. My kids grew up, and they now understand why I joined the military. I have a relationship with my granddaughter, and her name is FAITH. Won't He do it!

Everything is not perfect, but I am still working daily at being better than yesterday. I was believing I needed to hear someone tell me I can do it. I can fix it. I can push through. The entire time all I needed to do was believe in myself and tell myself those things. When you have done your best, it's good enough for you, and it's good enough for everyone else. I was so hard on myself. I wanted to blame people for my being alone. And myself, for getting hurt. I didn't understand what I did wrong; my kids did not like me. It's just life. There are things we have no control over.

Take care of yourself. Do what you can within reason and compliment yourself. I had to stop saying I didn't have anyone. I just didn't reach out to anyone. I had to stop thinking just because I was a giver and loved making people happy, it didn't mean everyone was going to be like me. I stopped assuming people would be like I was. I learned to say no, instead of yes. I tried to think more before acting. I listened when people talked more instead of waiting for my turn to talk. Sometimes, our personalities have a way of affecting our daily life and how we handle things in the real world.

Times are still hard. Things are sometimes challenging. I am still disabled. The only difference is that now, I know who I am, and I don't let anyone tell me how far I can go. I know that it can look like you can't win and seem bound to lose everything but stay in the race, even if you finish last. At least, You Finished. Live life and be grateful even for the little things.

No one can tell your story better than you. It's like a movie. You want to know what happens in the end. Stick around because you earned your testimony and without life's tests, you would not have a "testistory"! If you get STUCK, we will come to get you somehow some way, they came and got me.

I had to tell this story, and I thank God for Faydria Fox and Chivaughnn P. Smith for supporting and encouraging me and Terri Williams for the continued support. I give my continued respect, love, and appreciation to the Honorable Noreen N. Henry, who cares enough to create this powerful movement of strong and inspirational individuals that want you to know that if we can make it, so can you and so will You! For My Angel Jesse Earl & My Butterfly Elaine Majoni.

How did I overcome it? I accepted situations, asked for help, and never gave up.

Army Strong Built FORD Tough

Tracey Ford

Sergeant Tracey Ford a.k.a Laweziana is a Louisiana native by way of Texas. She is a retired U.S. Army Veteran with twelve active-duty years and had served in Operation Iraqi Freedom/Operation Enduring Freedom. She has worked with Counter Drug Task Force & Team Engineer, and she was a lead Non-Commissioned Safety Officer with Team Shield. She was also appointed as the Lieutenant Colonel's Driver. She is a Wounded Warrior and has received many honorable awards and medals such as the Combat War Medal.

Tracey is the CEO and owner of Laweziana Dance Fitness. Her professional dance career has spanned more than twenty years. She is a Certified State National Presenter of Dance and teaches a variety of dance formats. She also works for Music Recording Artist CUPID, teaching Curobiks as a Master Trainer.

In 2004, she was severely injured in Iraq and became permanently disabled. The doctors told her she would never walk again, let alone dance, but she clearly defied the odds. To this day she continues to undergo surgeries and medical procedures periodically. Despite it all, she has committed herself to travel across the world while helping others reach their health & fitness goals by motivating them through her LOVE & PASSION for DANCE!!

Tracey continues to give back to her country by volunteering to work with her local police departments and by sponsoring youth recreation teams. She also dedicates her life to taking care of her mother while faithfully driving eleven hours every two weeks to provide hands-on care. As if her life has not already been challenging, she sold her home and became homeless so that she could make sure to provide for her mom.

Although Tracey has faced many obstacles in life, she continues to persevere and is a constant inspiration to everyone she meets.

Connect with Tracey "Laweziana" Ford: https://linktr.ee/LawezianaDanceFitness

CHAPTER 9
I Had to Choose Me
Nicole Rhone

Are you the "one" or the "go-to" in your family, friendship, and work circles? When I say "the one," I mean the person who always picks up the phone to be a listening ear and give solutions. The person who stays late and takes on extra projects at work to pull off the impossible. The one who sacrifices their needs to show up and be there for others, even when you don't want to. If that sounds familiar, this is for you.

If you're wondering how I know you so well yet have never met you, it's because I've been in your shoes. I'm a mom, a wife, a big sister to nine siblings (second in command since I'm the first daughter), a business owner who left the corporate world after twenty years to pursue my purpose, and a woman who knows what it's like to wear many hats. Like you, I consider myself a driven, high-achieving woman who knows how to overcome obstacles that cross my path, and that's because I watched my parents make it through addiction, poverty, and unhealthy relationships. Through that exposure, I learned to take pride in "beating the odds." After all, I was the first "one" to graduate from college and get a master's degree. I was the first "one" to make six figures, marry, have kids, and break glass ceilings. Because of that, I was also the "one" that everybody leaned on. When you think about it, that's a lot of weight to carry, but when you do it for so long and do it well, it becomes the norm *and* a badge of honor.

What I didn't realize, though, was being there for everyone, pushing myself to show up no matter how I felt, and high-achieving was something I was addicted to. I used it as a coping mechanism. I didn't know it then, but I liked being needed – it made me feel good. And I liked being busy – it made me feel important. It also helped me not have to deal with my emotions.

Every woman I admired growing up was always busy, put others before themselves, and seemed to wear what I viewed as a superwoman cape at all times. I watched women work themselves to the bone while neglecting themselves to have a successful career or keep friends and family around. I watched my mom, aunts, and good friends stay in unhealthy relationships "for the kids." I unknowingly internalized that and believed it's what you're *supposed* to do. From my mom to women like Claire Huxtable on the Cosby show – doing it all and doing it with a smile is what I thought being a "good" wife and mom, and overall, every good woman was all about.

I felt like that for a very long time until January of 2019 to be exact. By then, I'd achieved what I considered "success" in my personal and professional life. After graduating from college, I quickly climbed the corporate ladder in my career, even after becoming a single mom at 18 years old, and made more money than I'd ever imagined. At this point, my husband and I had been married for six years, had two children, the nice house in the suburbs, the cute dog… everything that looked and seemed picture-perfect. To everyone outside, it looked like I was living the dream. But the truth is, I was exhausted, unfulfilled, battling severe depression and anxiety, and secretly suffering in silence. I felt like what my mentor, Patrice Washington, calls a public success and a private failure.

Nobody knew the six-figure job I mentioned was more toxic than rat poisoning, and I was commuting four hours per day to and from work. Yes, I basically had a part-time job traveling just to have a job! Crazy, right? Because of that, I barely saw my children outside of drop off and pick up, let alone made it to important school events. Since I was exhausted by the time I walked in the door every day, I came in angry, mean, and not showing up as the mom I wanted to be. I justified it by saying, "I'm giving you all the things I never had," or "You should be grateful for how hard I work."

The six-year marriage I talked about was even worse. Although we looked like the perfect, happy couple to those around us, the reality was our marriage was in shambles. For years, I'd been hiding from close friends and family that my husband was an alcoholic. He'd been fired from at least two jobs, received several DUI's which resulted in losing his driving privileges, and I could no longer travel for business without worrying about if he would stay sober in my absence.

So while my career and professional life were soaring, my personal life was a hot mess! Even with all that happening in the background, I showed up to work smiling like nothing was wrong. I kept showing up for people around me, adding more to my plate than my capacity could handle, and I used it to bury my feelings by keeping myself busy. When people asked me how I was doing, I did what most of us do and said things like "Everything is fine" or "I'm great, how are you?" to take the spotlight off myself. I kept it up, until one day I couldn't. The one place I was always successful at work started to crumble. I found myself frequently overpromising and under-delivering. I was missing deadlines, coming to work looking disheveled, and producing work that was mediocre at best.

When I realized that things were starting to unravel in my safe space, I decided taking a trip to Florida to get some relaxation would do the trick – so I booked a long weekend for my birthday. I just *knew* all I needed was a mini-vacation with a good girlfriend, and I'd be fixed. Like magic, right? On that trip, I decided to open up to my friend about what was happening in my marriage, how stressed I was, and that I felt like I was falling apart. To my surprise, her response to my vulnerability was, "Girl, you should be lucky you *have* a husband." I thought maybe she didn't hear me, or I didn't explain it right, so I tried saying it in a different way. Her response was still the same, but this time more frustrating. When I said, "I'm hurting, and being at this toxic job and in this unhealthy marriage is killing me." She said, "Girl, at least he has a job, and you make good money. I *wish* I was in your shoes". Needless to say, I kept my mouth closed about what was going on in my life for the rest of the trip. Thank God it was only a three-day trip because I was devastated and felt crazy for saying anything at all after that. It made me question, was it *that* bad? Was I being ungrateful and dramatic?

What I felt in that moment and days after I got home confirmed my reason for secretly struggling in the first place – that nobody understood what I was going through and that since I was "the one" to help everyone else, I'd never get the support I needed anyway. I told myself this was no different since I'd overcome so many other obstacles on my own. I went back to being busy, suppressing my feelings, and being on autopilot.

What happened next is something I didn't see coming at all. As mentioned, I went back to business as usual, commuting four hours a day, stressing about my personal and professional life, and going through the motions. This time though, something was off. Something was different, and I couldn't put my finger on it. A week after my mini-vacation, as I commuted to work one morning, I started feeling these unusual pains in my arms, simply from walking to and from my office or even sitting at my desk typing. Although I noticed the pain, it wasn't *horrible*, so I chalked it up to getting back in the swing of things after being out the week before. By the next day, my pain increased and spread to my legs. Instead of addressing it, I kept trying to rationalize it. Have you ever done that before? By the end of the week, I was in even more pain, and while chatting it up about weekend plans, I told my co-worker about it, and she suggested I get checked out. Of course, I dismissed her recommendation, tried to ignore my body's signals, and kept doing what I did best – staying busy. When I got home that night, I tried taking Ibuprofen, taking a long hot shower, and even got a massage, hoping it would ease the pain, but nothing worked. By Saturday morning, I could barely move. It was so bad that I remember coming down the stairs from my bedroom, making it to the couch, and bursting into tears. My entire body felt like it was on fire. I couldn't even breathe without being in pain. At that moment, my daughter, who was 14 years old then, walked into the room and said, "Mommy, what's wrong?" I replied, "I have no idea, but I'm in so much pain I can't move." She said, "Can you please go to the hospital? I'm worried about you." When I saw the look on her face, I tried to push through the pain and pretend it wasn't as bad as it was. I said, "You know what, I'm just gonna go upstairs and lay down. I'll go if I don't feel better in a few hours." She looked me in my eyes as I wiped away tears and said, "Mom, I've watched you try to do everything to feel better, but nothing is working. Now you're sitting here crying because you're in so much pain, and you wanna go upstairs and lay down? That doesn't make any sense. I know you're the parent, but I'm taking you to the hospital."

After that heart-to-heart conversation, I burst into tears again because she was right. I *needed* to go, but I was thinking, what am I gonna tell them… that I have pain all over my body? They're gonna think I'm crazy. Despite those thoughts, I listened to my baby and allowed her to take me. Now you might be thinking, what, you let your 14-year-old drive you?!?! Honestly, I was in so much pain that I wouldn't have been able to drive anyway. It was so bad that she had to help me get dressed, so I could get out of the house! On top of that, my husband was intoxicated and didn't have a license, so I figured her driving me was essential.

Luckily, the hospital was less than a mile away and on the same street we lived on, just three blocks away.

Shortly after getting to the hospital, I explained my symptoms, they ran tests, and I sent my daughter home. Within thirty minutes, the doctor came in saying that I was not only being admitted but also being rushed to ICU because my life was in danger due to an extremely high CPK level, which measures the amount of protein in your blood. I can't even begin describing the paralyzing fear I felt at that moment.

After being admitted and whisked away to ICU, they explained that my muscles were breaking down and depositing protein into my blood. So much so that I was at risk for kidney failure, my heart was inflamed, and the rest of my organs started shutting down. Apparently, a normal CPK level measures around 50 to 100 units. My level was measuring over two hundred thousand. Yeah, you read that right! **Two. Hundred. Thousand.** The number was so high that they didn't tell me at first because they didn't want me to panic, which might increase the number. Because they weren't sure what was causing my muscles to break down, the only thing they could do was pump liters of fluid through me, which compromised my already enlarged heart and lungs, but it was the only option.

To say that the doctors were confused is an understatement. They ran every test possible, had the infectious disease people called in, and kept ordering scans of my entire body. Still, they couldn't understand how or why I, a healthy young woman with no previous health issues, had symptoms identical to someone who'd been crushed by falling concrete and left for days. They said it was as if I'd been in a violent car accident and had broken every bone in my body. Every doctor constantly told me that they'd never, in their 30-year medical careers, EVER seen anything like this. After asking all the questions they could think of, one of the doctors asked if there was anything stressful going on in my life. Because you've read this far, you already know the answer to that. At that moment, I heard a small, still voice saying, "Be honest." I opened up a little – mind you, I didn't know this doctor from a can of paint, so I shared minimal information – but with what I did share, she said, "Whatever you're dealing with, the stress and amount of pressure you're under is manifesting in physical form in your body. If you want to live, you have to choose yourself. Had you waited just

15 minutes, you would have died. I'm glad you listened to your daughter because she saved your life."

Think about that for a second. I was told that my body was responding to my mental and emotional anguish in a physical form. I'd heard it was possible, but never in a million years did I think suppressing my feelings, secretly struggling, and being everything to everybody would take a toll on me like that. Like most of us, when faced with life-altering circumstances, I prayed, asked God to heal me, and promised if my health were restored, I'd do whatever He said to do. What I heard was, "You have to trust Me." I didn't fully know what it meant at the time, but what it turned out to be was that I had to surrender my stress to God.

Throughout my week in ICU, I constantly asked God for guidance. I realized that my marriage, my job, and not taking care of myself were literally killing me and that I had to make some tough decisions and immediate changes in my life. I was at what I call maximum capacity. Capacity is the amount of time, energy, and resources available to handle all the moving pieces of your life. And because I'd been running on empty for so long, my body could no longer handle it. I was maxed out with no capacity even to keep my body functioning. Once my condition improved, I vowed to teach every woman I could find about the importance of capacity and how to manage it, so that they didn't end up in the hospital fighting for their lives as I did. That's how I became the Capacity Coach and created what I call the keys to managing your capacity: awareness, alignment, and action. I used those keys to identify what was essential, shift my priorities, and take action to get unstuck.

Moving by faith and definitely not by sight, I was released from the hospital after deciding in my heart and mind that it was time to step back from my marriage. I knew that if I didn't, I'd end up right back in ICU, or even worse, dead. I had to have an honest conversation with myself about what was working and what was not. And then take the necessary steps to put me first.

Having all that time to just be, without being busy, solving other people's problems or working, I realized I'd been holding on to my marriage because I was afraid to be alone. Yes, I loved my husband and honored our vows too, but the truth was, I was embarrassed about looking like a failure to the people around me and ashamed to be a single parent again at 35 years old. I kept thinking, how would it look if the woman who makes six figures and has this picture-perfect life admits it's not-so-perfect? What are my friends and family going to think? What does that say about me as a woman? How can I possibly do this by myself? Is this what's best for my husband or my children? Will the kids blame me for breaking up our family? Will my husband be okay – how will he be able to support himself? So many thoughts and questions raced through my head.

Despite my fear and all those feelings, I kept my word to God to trust Him, and the day I was released from the hospital, I told my husband we needed to separate, and I wanted him to move out. It was one of the hardest things I've ever had to do in my life, but I knew it was essential. I had to choose me. If I didn't, I would remain stuck, and my children would lose their mother. I didn't want to keep playing the "fake it till you make it" game. I didn't want to keep being busy for the sake of being busy, so I didn't have to deal with my feelings. I didn't want to solve everyone else's problems or be the "one" anymore. My priorities were to be healthy, have peace, and thrive, not just survive. But to do that, I had to choose myself. And I did. For the first time in my life, I started to make decisions based on what *I* needed rather than what was best for everyone else. If I wanted to live, I had to stop worrying about other people's thoughts and perceptions of me. None of that mattered, and once I realized it, my choices and actions became aligned.

It wasn't easy, and I was scared out of my mind. I had no idea how it would pan out, but I had faith that everything would work itself out, and I believed it. Making that *one* decision was one of the best things I've ever done, and it caused a ripple effect in my personal and professional life. Because I was now aware of my capacity and made decisions based on that capacity, I began having the courage and strength to let go of what was no longer serving me and put me first. Doing so in my marriage gave me the confidence to make changes at work. I knew the job I had at the time was unhealthy, but before my hospital stay, I believed I wouldn't be able to find a job that would pay me as much in the suburbs. I believed I had to work in the city to make "good" money. But after rinsing and repeating what I applied to my marriage, I used those same keys of managing my capacity – awareness, alignment, and action – and applied the same level of faith, mindset shift, and belief in my career. About a month after separating from my husband, I was offered a role that was not only fifteen minutes from my house; it also came with a twenty-thousand-dollar increase.

After changing my marriage and career, I started to make changes in every other area of my life including friendships. One of my favorite quotes I hope you will use after reading this chapter is "To be aware is to be alive", and it's my hope that awareness will help you in your journey.

Now I'm glad I'm here to tell the story today, but as I mentioned, I had to get honest about what was and was not working in my life. I can't tell you that managing your capacity, choosing to put yourself first, and making uncomfortable but necessary decisions will be a cakewalk. It will not. In fact, it'll likely be the exact opposite. But are you willing to pay the cost of staying stuck, or are you ready to do what it takes to put yourself first?

What I want you to take from my experience is that when you are doing all the things including dealing with your relationships, working your butt off, and being the "one" to everyone around you, it takes a toll on your capacity.

The problem is, too many of us don't realize we're at max capacity *until* we end up with health, relationship, or financial issues. And most of us are the high-achieving ones this happens to. That's because we're so accustomed to making stuff happen and doing so at the sacrifice of our wellbeing. We look good on paper, on Instagram, and Facebook but secretly struggle with overwhelm, mental exhaustion, and burnout. At the end of the day, you have a choice, even when it feels like you don't. Stuck doesn't have to continue to be your story. What are you going to choose?

Nicole Rhone

Nicole Rhone is the CEO of Flourishing, LLC, which is a coaching and consulting company that helps high-performing women and businesses increase their capacity for sustainable success. She is also the host of the five-star rated Flow and Flourish Podcast, an international Diversity, Equity and Inclusion trainer, as well as a highly sought-after Capacity Coach.

She's been featured on the NBC Today Show, Soigne + Swank Magazine, ABC7 Chicago, Redefining Wealth Community with Patrice Washington, Chicago Parent Magazine, and numerous podcasts around the world as a leader and influencer who helps women create balance between their personal and professional lives.

This wife and mother of two spent over a decade as a coach and human resources leader in the corporate sector, supporting thousands of employees globally, so she knows what it's like to wear many hats and juggle competing priorities.

Nicole has worked for and partnered with billion-dollar, Fortune 500 companies such as BMO Harris Bank, Roosevelt University, and Northwestern Medicine to help them coach employees, build leadership capabilities, and cultivate thriving company cultures.

Because of her more than twenty years of corporate experience, Nicole understands the unique challenges of busy, high-performing women as well as growing businesses, and how a lack of fluidity can create a barrier between them and their next level. Her mantra is, "When you flow effortlessly, you flourish tremendously."

For more information, check out her website at www.nicolerhone.com, or connect with her on Facebook @Nicole Rhone and on Instagram @Nicole_Rhone.

CHAPTER 10
Overcome F.E.A.R. to R.I.S.E.
Latika Vines

When I was 16 years old, I made the persuaded decision to dedicate my life to being a Jehovah's Witness. My mother and siblings were Jehovah's Witnesses and the influence around me provoked that decision, although I was still unsure of who God was. I knew that He was real, but I never was taught how to have a personal and intimate relationship with Him. So, when I was baptized, sparks did not fly, and my life did not change as I expected. In fact, I began to experience trauma for the next few years.

By the age of 19 years old, I became a wife and stepmother to two children, who were old enough to be my little sisters. I barely knew who I was, and I quickly had to learn how to be a wife - a wife to a man who was raised in a different religion and culture than I, and who was 13 years my senior. Again, I made this decision unsure of who I was and what my future was going to be. And it caused me to listen, watch, and submit to the influences around me.

Now, you may be thinking that I made some crazy decisions in my teenage years – but who hasn't? You may not have gotten married as a teenager, but what decision has caused you to look back and reflect, questioning your critical thinking skills? I'm sure there are plenty of decisions you could list.

My marriage was not horrible, at first. We had a beautiful baby girl within two years; however, after she was born, there was an inclination inside of me to become a better person (I knew that I was ordained to do more in life than be a wife and be in a mediocre job). Again, my upbringing was very religious and that was all I knew. Also, I was going to church with my then-husband. So, I began going back to being a Jehovah's Witness and all that went along with that decision (i.e., not celebrating holidays, not fellowshipping with those who were not Jehovah's Witnesses, etc....). And it caused a war in my household.

Unfortunately, our daughter died of sudden infant death syndrome (SIDS), when she was seven months and twenty-nine days old. At the tender age of 21 years old, I began the divorce proceedings to separate from my then-husband. I never imagined that I would be starting my adult life in this manner. But when one makes decisions that will have a life-long impact, you never sit down to think about your future first.

Being 21 years old, divorced, and carrying a story of burying my only child, I was told to keep quiet. I was told that no one wanted to hear my "sob story" or even know that I experienced such trauma in my life. And the fear inside caused me to only let certain people know what I went through – and those individuals couldn't help me. For a few years, I was muted, and I allowed myself to accept that muteness, because I made the decision to allow fear to overrule me. I allowed the fear of what others thought of me to overrule me. I allowed the fear of what others would say about me to overrule me. I allowed the fear of being a 21-year-old divorced woman, without a college degree overrule me. I allowed the fear of my story to hold me in bondage. I was fearful of using my voice to tell my story. I was stuck!

- *Have you allowed your story to keep you in bondage and stuck?*
- *Have you allowed your story to make you feel ashamed for the decisions you made in life?*
- *Have you allowed fear to keep your story muted?*
- *Have you allowed fear to prevent you from experiencing the blessings that are destined for your life?*
- *Have you allowed fear to keep you stuck in your story, not able to break free?*

Esther was Obedient in Using Her Voice

As I reflect on my own life decisions and how I allowed others to mute my purpose, I am reminded of Esther. Her story begins with both of her parents dying and being adopted by her uncle, Mordecai. The bible tells us that "she was admired by everyone who saw her." (Esther 1:15 NLT) In fact, it was her beauty, not where she came from, that caught the eye of the King's trusted advisor, Haman, and later she became one of the King's wives. Fast forward, Haman, did not like the lack of respect (Haman's definition of respect) Mordecai showed him, so he "tricked" the King in signing a decree to get rid of anyone from Jewish decent; this would also include Esther who is a Jew. (Esther 3:8-10, NLT)

Once Esther learned of the decree, she had to make a hard decision – she could keep silent and die with her people or say something to her husband to save her people.

Mordecai advises Esther to mention the new decree to the King; but the rule is to never approach the King without permission and those who don't follow that rule are put to death. At first, she allowed the rule set by her husband to prevent her from speaking up. But, after seeking guidance from Mordecai and being obedient to God, she was able to approach her husband and save her people, by speaking up and using her voice. (Esther 4:13-17, NLT)

To better understand what occurred, let's break it down:

- *Esther went before the King (her husband) to make an appeal for her people.*
- *Esther was obedient to what God called her to do.*
- *In Esther's obedience, God covered her life.*
- *God used Esther to save His people.*

Haman allowed his power to overrule the Jewish people, which forced Esther to believe that she had to be mute. What has occurred in your life that has forced you to believe you have to be mute?

When you look at Esther's story, she suffered trauma in her life. Both of her parents died, and she was raised by her uncle. Can you relate to her story? But, because she was raised by a man who loved her and treated her as his own daughter, she became a bride to the King. And with the wisdom from Mordecai, she was able to overcome her fear. But how?

I F.E.A.R. Not

Both Esther and I had to understand that F.E.A.R. doesn't overrule us. Let's break down what F.E.A.R. is and how you can overcome it:

F: Forget

As I mentioned, I grew up in a very religious household, so I was taught to be fearful in an unhealthy way, which I carried into my adulthood. I was fearful of what others would say about my story and what they would think of me. Esther was fearful of the rules that kept her mute. But both Esther and I had to forget what people say about us; and forget the negative things we said about ourselves. I can only imagine Esther had personal conversations with herself, trying to rationalize what her uncle told her and what she knew of the King. And I'm sure she cried herself to sleep asking God, "Why her?" Have you ever asked yourself that question? I have questioned God why my daughter died and why I had to experience the pain of losing her. I questioned God why He let me marry so young to only experience pain. But that feeling of being alone, empty, and doubtful was from the rules set by others. Will you continue to allow the rules of others to prevent you from being victorious?

E: Everything

I had to realize that everything I went through was for someone else to receive the victory. By sharing my story and allowing my purpose to overrule my feelings (and the feelings of others), I was able to understand that I was and continue to be a vessel, so that I can build His kingdom. If Esther hadn't used her voice, what would have happened to the Jewish people in her day? If I don't continue to use my voice, what mother or lost 21-year-old girl would continue to suffer in silence? Will you continue to allow everything you went through to keep you silent? Someone is waiting to hear your story and learn how to overcome their own. You have no idea who is attached to your story.

A: And

From Esther's story, we were taught that not everyone will come with you to the next chapter of your story. Haman was caught, and his power was taken away from him. Likewise, I got divorced and received a new set of friends and loved ones who supported the next chapters of my story. You can not bring everyone with you on the next chapter of your story. You do not have an "AND" on this journey. God is your partner. God is your guidance. God will give you the discernment on what and where to go and who to talk to. You will not and cannot bring some friends, associates, and/or family members that are not ready to hear, acknowledge, apologize, and move forward in your story. Will you continue to hold onto past relationships, disappointments, and trauma that are preventing you from reaching victory?

R: Run

I couldn't continue to run from telling my story and learning from it. And Esther couldn't run from being a Jew and saving her people. The lives of her people were left in her hands. As you reflect on your story, remember that you cannot continue to run from your destiny. When you run, you become tired, lose direction, and miss your blessings, victory, freedom, and joy. Will you continue to run from where you are supposed to go?

Begin to R.I.S.E.

Esther and I had to set aside fear to be obedient to what was next in our stories. What about you? It is time for you to Respond Intentionally Serving in Excellence or R.I.S.E. Let's outline how you can R.I.S.E.:

R: Respond

Reflect on Esther's story where fear initially kept her from going to her husband to save her people. To save herself and her people, she had to respond to the destiny or calling that was on her life. Likewise, you must accept that your story existed and respond to the call to carry out what God has destined over your life. Your story was on a rollercoaster, but you survived that scary ride because God was with you.

I: Intentionally

After losing my daughter and going through a failed marriage, I felt like I lost at life. And, when I went back to college, all my research papers were written about my daughter, the risk factors of SIDS, and the impact death causes to mothers. In fact, one of my professors expressed to me that I had to move on from writing about my daughter, because he believed that it was impossible to continue talking about death. But what I realized was that although my professor was tired of me talking about my story, I had to be intentional to share it with others. He may not have been my audience to hear it, but my other professors appreciated it. I will always remember the one professor who sent me an email, after I submitted a paper on Infant Mortality sharing his own story of how he lost his daughter to SIDS. Not everyone will have the privilege to understand your story, but you must be intentional in sharing your story with those who will learn from it and/or understand it.

You also must be intentional with spending time with God to let go of the fear you have allowed yourself to accept and hold onto. God tells us that we are not made to fear anything, but to have power. (2 Timothy 1:17, NLT). You hold the power to RISE!

You must be intentional in:

- *Spending time with God in prayer – what time can you dedicate to prayer?*
- *Spending time with God reading the Bible – what time can you dedicate to reading?*
- *Spending time with God in praise and worship – what time can you dedicate to praise and worship?*
- *Spending time with God hearing his confirmations, wisdom, and discernment – what time can you dedicate to meditate and hear His voice?*

S: Serving

Esther's obedience served her people. My obedience in telling my story served those who suffered a loss of a child, went through a divorce at an early age, married young, or are now understanding the purpose behind their story. Your story will serve the people that you are attached to through your calling. But, by neglecting to serve, you are neglecting the peace, freedom, and joy that people need to survive their own stories. Along with that, you are neglecting the peace, freedom, and joy you can experience by letting go and serving others.

It took me years to understand that my story is one of service; that I am only a vessel who is needed to help, heal, and direct people to the love and grace of God. What service will you provide by sharing your story? What service will you provide by overcoming the fear of accepting and acknowledging your story? What service will you provide by being intentional with spending time with God and accepting the call on your life? How will you serve your people?

E: Excellence

When Esther understood her assignment, she used wisdom to walk and act in decency and order. Although fear initially prevented her from saying something to her husband, the guidance and love from her uncle allowed her to be excellent in delivering a hard message – her assignment. When it is time for you to overcome fear to accept, acknowledge, and share your story, do so in excellence. Listen to the breadcrumbs from God, giving you the direction on where, who, and what you should say and do. Not everyone needs to hear your story or feel your pain; but only those who are destined to need to. Surround yourself with individuals who can give you wisdom, who can pray with you and over you, and who you can be vulnerable with while accepting, acknowledging, and sharing your story.

As you reflect on Esther's story, she experienced trauma early in her life. And, although fear initially prevented her from speaking up and telling her husband about where she came from and what was going to happen to her people, she was able to overcome and R.I.S.E. No matter what trauma you experienced in your story, you too can overcome and R.I.S.E. You must believe that your story is for someone else to receive the victory, just like you received the victory. You must believe that your story is not over. Like Esther, you will move on and do great things, including saving the lives of others attached to your story. Remember to F.E.A.R. not and R.I.S.E.

"God did not give you the spirit of F.E.A.R." - 1 Timothy 1:17 ESV

All Scriptural References mentioned are taken from the *Holy Bible*, New Living Translation, copyright © 1996, 2004, 2015 by Tyndale House Foundation. All rights reserved.

Latika Vines

Latika Vines is a Baltimore, Maryland native, currently residing in the Southern part of the state with her husband and four young daughters. Latika empowers working mothers, in male-dominated industries, to lead and grow in their Careers while strengthening Organizations to retain them. Latika is a firm believer that everyone has a career vision, and although that vision can get blurry and put on the backburner at times, it must be picked back up and turned into an initiative (ACTION)! She teaches working mothers how to do so by being the B.O.S.S. of their Careers.

As an 5x Author, Career Development Strategist/People Developer and Work-Life Balance Advocate & Educator, and CEO, Visionary Initiatives, LLC, Latika partners with Tech, Law Enforcement, and Professional Services Organizations to develop their Workforce, particularly their Working Mothers, through Career Development Workshops, Strategies, and Coaching to increase Employee Satisfaction, Improve Productivity and Retention and Career Mobility. Additionally, Latika is the host of The Latika Vines Show, a work and life balance podcast for working moms.

Latika has over sixteen years of Career/Workforce Development and Learning & Development experience and has been certified in Human Capital Strategist and Strategic Workforce Planning from Human Capital Institute, and

Performance Consulting for Trainers from The Training Clinic. Latika has also received her certificate in Women Entrepreneurship from Cornell University.

In addition to growing her career and empire, Latika is the International Association of Women - Waldorf Chapter President, providing mentorship and guidance to women in the Southern Maryland area to achieve their life, career and business goals.

For advice on career mobility strategies for your organization or to have Latika facilitate Team Building, Strategic Planning, or HR related workshops for your leaders, please contact her at info@visionary-initiatives.com.

Download the complimentary bi-monthly Career Development Resource Newsletter at https://www.visionary-initiatives.com/newsletter.

Learn more about Visionary Initiatives at www.visionary-initiatives.com

Listen to The Latika Vines Show at https://podcasts.apple.com/us/podcast/the-latika-vines-show/id1497895539

Connect with Latika

www.facebook.com/visionaryinitiatives | www.linkedin/in/latika-s-vines | www.twitter.com/latika_vines

CHAPTER 11
Stuck Is Not My Story, I Overcame (Playing the Victim)
Priscilla C. Baldwin

My name is Priscilla, and as I look at the title of this book, it puts me in a whirlwind of emotions concerning my life with its many stories and victories as well. We never know what lies ahead of us or the pitfalls underneath us. We are told to keep our heads up, and we strive to do so every time not knowing the outcome yet believing with our whole hearts. That is faith.

As I have become a mature woman aging gracefully, I look back over some crazy situations in my life, when I thought and believed I was right and everybody else was wrong as wrong could be (I was playing the victim, it was them or him but never me).

When playing the victim, you get lost in it and it's hard as hell to find your way back to reality. The REAL reality, not the one that you tell yourself. Being the victim puts you in the position to have "Yes" people around you, and if you find yourself in their presence, please "RUN", for they are doing your frame of mind and relationships a disservice.

The victim mentality brings a lot of pain, unforgiveness, resentment, self-doubt, hatred, low self-esteem, and lack of trust towards others and yourself. You begin to stop trusting YOUR judgment on issues where it was easy, and now, it's just difficult. It spreads into other areas of your life and seeps through the very core of your being.

You don't see it and how it affects you and your surroundings, relationships, and friendships. You're blinded to the change that has occurred within you. The victim mentality is something that you must be aware of. Looking back, it was subtle. I got so caught up in the pain of the story that I didn't care who heard it as long they saw me and the pain that I was in. The re- telling of it somehow was not enough. It was reliving it and overthinking it that was causing me issues of self-doubt.

Boy Meets Girl

So, here's the story, "Boy meets Girl. They fall in love. The girl gets pregnant, then they get married. Simple story, right? Maybe? Two young people got married due to circumstances (Because my Mama said so) and who is to argue with her? Certainly, NOT ME OR HIM. You had to know her, lol.

The beginning years were great. We were walking into adulthood. I was 20 and he was 22. We were finding our way together with baggage from our childhood and the other baggage that we were creating. Truth be told, I lived a sheltered life. Having older parents, I was very naive about certain things.

I dated my high school sweetheart. He was a track star, and all the girls liked him. He was very popular; he could get any girl he wanted and half the time, he did. He was a persuasive talker, and he loved a good time being social with his friends. He was the big dog on campus, so I thought. He would tell you what you wanted to hear so sincerely, when he spoke with you. He still does. We both played the victim to a certain degree.

Growing into adulthood was not easy. The responsibility was a nightmare. To be honest, learning to navigate motherhood and being a wife was a lot for me and adding five more people to be responsible for was just WOW. Mother of six, keep up, lol, wouldn't change a thing about those people in my life. Catch me on a good day, those thoughts may change, lol. I can honestly say that we both were victims of our environment, family, social status, and so much more.

When they say that we're a product of our environment, we are. I expected him to be a person that he couldn't be. It is not that he didn't try, but he couldn't be who I needed him to be. I see that now it took years to see it, the extramarital affairs and our toxic relationship. My being passive aggressive didn't help the situation. I remember letting situations build up and getting so mad and exploding into a rage and being physical with him, but he was NEVER physical with me. There was verbal and mental aggression on both our parts. What I do know is **"Hurt people hurt others."** It's true.

Years after the divorce there was still resentment, hatred, self-doubt, low self-esteem, and a lot of blaming in the marriage with my ex-husband. And his actions at times were tit for tat petty things. The people we loved the most, our children were getting hurt and looking at our treatment of each other. It's with hindsight that I saw this. I didn't see this when I was being the victim and I was making sacrifices for my children. Telling them everything I did and pointing out his flaws or his inconsistencies, which was not right, or just wanting them to see what I did for them, so that they would love me and not him. My actions concerning this was totally wrong. Who am I to tell my children who to love, especially their father? Can you see how this spills over to every area of my life? Being the victim is no joke. It overtakes you. If you're not careful, you could slip into depression and become bitter as well.

The Badge of Victimhood

An example of this would be the time that my younger children were in an after-school program in elementary school. I was wearing the Badge of Victim with honor for some reason. I also was wearing bitterness, resentment, **and** hurt. Sarcasm was my top-notch reaction. I was the bag lady in the song by "Erykah Badu" with the emotional baggage that I didn't know how to let go of. I knew how to react **but** not respond, and there is a big difference. We react out of our emotions **or** feelings. We respond when we have learned to take a step back, think it through, then speak with a profound answer.

With my being a reactive person, the workers at the after-school program were very curt with me. I didn't imagine that. Looking back, I can see what they saw. They saw a large black woman who was passive-aggressive. In fact, more aggressive than passive at times. Being offensive at more times than I can count (caught up in the daily life of surviving) with no excuses for such behavior. All I could see was me and my issues, trying to keep my head above water or so I thought.

Let's fast forward several years. The same children are now in high school, and I am working for a mental health facility in my small town as a Behavior

Technician at a behavioral school. This particular afternoon I was turning in some paperwork and had to pass by a group of people that were smoking outside. I was walking pass this group, and a young lady asks a question, "Aren't you… she mentions my son's name, and I smile and said yes. She proceeds to tell me who she is (she was one of the after-school workers, when they were in elementary school). I continue with the conversation, getting caught up on what they were doing in school.

As I was heading back to my car going down the street, I heard the Holy Spirit tell me that I needed to apologize. In my mind, apologize for what. I went the following day to look for the young lady, but she wasn't there, The day after that, she still wasn't there. I left the campus and called my spiritual mother Leila Morris at the time and told her what happened. She said maybe I just needed to show that I was obedient to what was being said to me. On the third day, I went back to the campus of the facility, and she was there, I did apologize to her about my actions during that time in my life, and what she said after that blew me away. She accepted my apology and stated that it's okay, because when the Director or Assistant Director saw me coming, they didn't want to have anything to do with me and left her to deal with me then. This hit me like a ton of bricks. I explained that I wasn't the same person, and that I'm not like that anymore. I think she halfheartedly believed me.

I remember going to the car and crying to myself. And I kept saying that I'm not like that anymore. I don't know if it was more important for her to believe me or for me to believe myself, so that change had to come. My healing journey has been a long one, and I'm still healing. It is a "Lifestyle" and it's never-ending. Playing the victim will not get you an Oscar or an Emmy. If so, I think I would have won several times by now. As I sit thinking of playing the victim too many times, being offended had cost me relationships and friendships. Being misunderstood played a part as well. As stated, before, I didn't know how to let go of anything. I held grudges, which was not hurting the other people but me. I was my own worst enemy and held up my own blessings and progress/success. I had to learn to get out of my own way and do the inner work that I needed to be healed (to work on ME). The common denominator was me. Once I decided to do the work, it wasn't easy. It's hard to work on issues that you don't want to face or sit with. For me, sitting with it means meditating on it, feeling your emotions, figuring it out, accepting things or changing things for the better version of you. Healing requires a lot of work and self-reflection, praying, and dealing with your own demons. Your circle would be remembering the OLD you, while you continually change your response to them and other outside stimuli, which you fight with daily.

Trauma Bonds

Trauma bonds can be formed with others that have similar trauma or the same mindset as you. I found out that a lot of my relationships and friendships were trauma bonds, but I didn't know it at the time. I felt a closeness with an individual because of what we had gone through. I could relate to them when other people couldn't; they couldn't relate because they did not have the same trauma.

Trauma bonds can be researched on the internet. I thought that I was showing empathy to a certain person, but I really wasn't. What I saw was familiar; it was nothing that would sustain the friendship or relationship. There was nothing else in common but the trauma. For many years, I didn't know about trauma bonds. Many people are not aware that their friendships and relationships are based on this very thing. It puts you at a disadvantage because while you're thinking you have a real friendship, the truth is that each party needs to do some healing, seek therapy, and begin inner work on themselves. Playing the victim really opens the Pandora's box of emotions and the list goes on and on.

Codependency could be a part of it as well. It was for me. When I mentioned codependency, what was the first thing that came to your mind? Did you think drug addiction or alcoholism? When I would tell people about the book, they would look strangely at me. Having to explain the book and what it was about was a pain, but I wanted to share the information to make the load lighter for someone else. I received the book about codependency from a friend (She really was a friend, but I couldn't see it at the time, and we had a lot of miscommunications between us. She told me just like it was).

The book was "Codependent No More" by Melody Beattie. This was a great book because it was an eye opener for the behaviors that I thought was normal, if normal was real. In my opinion, there is no normal. My dysfunction may not be your dysfunction and vice versa. But we do have issues. A part of my codependency was I was a control freak. I wanted to control everything and everybody. An example would be when my children were middle schoolers or in high school, it had gotten to the point where they were not thinking for themselves. Others were rebellious, since I was taking away from them the ability to figure things out on their own by imposing my opinions and thoughts.

This behavior was exhausting, overwhelming, and uncalled for. I put myself in situations and circumstances that didn't concern me, and it felt like the weight of the world was on my shoulders. This allowed people to not develop coping skills or strategies for themselves, and I became the default person (go-to-person) I became Ms. Fix It, but after I began to work on me (inner work), I didn't want to fix people and things anymore. I started to resent it, but I caused it. I was thinking when you know better, you do better, I was BIG MAD.

When I started to pull back and let them handle their situation or not respond the way I always had, I was questioned, "Are you alright?" YUP, I'm still pulling back on some more things and don't get me wrong, this is a process, the healing journey. And the people you meet, make sure they are vetted. You don't want to waste time and energy on something that may turn out to be a trauma bond, since we're not choosing that anymore. We are actively listening to others and their pain but we're detaching ourselves from the pain and not coming in agreement with anything that no longer serves us.

The healing process is a lifestyle. It is not something that you do when you're in a situation; it's daily practice. During my healing process, I've learned so much about myself, and I'm still learning. My triggers and thought processes are sometimes on point. Then again, I ask myself "What were you thinking? lol. It's all a part of life and life's lessons. We either face them or not, it's our choice.

I chose to face my demons and work on me, good, bad, and the ugly. I've made some bad decisions and that's on me to clean up. I'm an imperfect person living in an imperfect world right along with the rest of humanity owning my stuff in the process which is a HUGE step for me. I've overcome playing the victim and owning my stuff like I said, but I also know when a person is playing the victim as well, manipulating the situation and the person. "Game know Game", as my sister-in-law likes to say, doesn't sit well with me because I did it.

You know the adage that the birds will come home to roost, they will or, in layman terms, your deeds will find you out; they do. Word of advice, "Don't play the victim, and don't be the victim." It works both ways. There are master manipulators out there. It could be you or someone you know. Isn't that how it works sometimes? Pandora's box is chaos, drama, and a feeling of hopelessness, which turns into a bottomless pit of circumstances.

Your healing will supply you with resources to work with and your very own arsenal to assist you when triggered or in a reactive state of mind (it's easy to be triggered, especially by individuals who know what buttons to push). Being in a responsive state of mind requires a lot of work, discipline, and the ability to be "quiet". My spiritual mother Leila Morris used to say that every question does not deserve an answer. I would tell you about the 3 F's, but that's another book, lol. My healing is on-going, and issues do still come up and I must be aware of what's being said and the emotional state of the person and myself. I choose to pick my battles, and not jump in headfirst.

Winning Battles, Not Wars

I've learned through my experiences that I did win the battle but lost the war, There's a difference. The difference is the battles that I won were small compared to the war. What I mean is the war is what cost me the price I didn't want to pay: friendships, relationships, and so much more.

As we grow in wisdom and in grace, we will learn going forward and hopefully not make the same mistakes. But if we do, we will reset, readjust, and keep on moving. There are so many twists and turns with being the victim but once you are free from it and over time when you're healed, you will see the pitfalls, chaos, drama, and destruction that you caused or that you contributed to in other people's lives as well as your own.

When I think of the deficits in me that playing the victim caused in my life, just imagine the ripple effect it caused with the lives that I touched daily. We impact people knowingly and unknowingly by our actions, reactions. We are responsible for our interactions with others whether it feels good or not. (Easier said than done). As we come near the end of this chapter, I hope that you will take the time to reflect on some of the things that were discussed and reflect on your life.

Hopefully something resonated with you whether you need to begin your healing process or that you will continue the journey as a lifestyle.

Life is too short to be held as a hostage in your own mind, your perceptions, limiting beliefs, misunderstanding, and, most importantly, people pleasing (those people don't care what you do as long as it lines up with their purpose). You limit your happiness based on others perception of you. Question why you are giving your power away to someone else? Yes, you are giving your power away, when you allow others to tell you about you and what you should be doing or not doing based on their perceptions.

Happiness is an inside job, and it's based largely on you, not outside stimuli. Seriously, if you base your happiness on a noun (person, place, or thing), you rob yourself of it. Your expectations set you up for disappointment. To be honest, you also set up the other person as well. The outcome of the projected expectation was not what you wanted, but that leaves the person in an unfavorable light with you, because it was your projected expectation onto the other person that make them responsible for your happiness which is a tall order and is not fair.

The expectation lies with you. You spend more time with yourself than you will ever spend with another individual (you can't run away from you). You should know yourself better than anyone else. I found myself doing this exact thing and was greatly disappointed every time, but it was my projected expectation that I put on others, making them responsible for what I expected them to do, which was not cool and it caused problems with me being upset, resentful, and frustrated when I started this mess, not knowing that I was making my own problems.

Nowadays, I try not to have expectations from people. I am learning to meet people where they are, not where I want them to be. The reason I am practicing this is that I got tired of being disappointed with the person, when in fact it was me projecting, so if I come with no expectations, I won't be disappointed and what needs to happen will happen organically (naturally). As I grow in grace and wisdom, I want to level up so that I won't be found where I started. This is a journey that I will fight daily. Sometimes, the old me shows its ugly head and I want to react and tell some people where to go and how to get there, if you know what I mean, but I have to step back and breathe, focus, and talk to myself. I have talked myself out of going to personally seeing that person. I do know how to navigate through it. It's just a hiccup- a reactive trigger for me.

Here are 3 tips:
1. Know your triggers and how they cause you to react; we are responding, not reacting.
2. Responding is taking a step back, breathing, and focusing
3. Speaking with a profound answer (this is my definition, and it keeps me focused and not crazy, lol).

I hope this has been an asset to you and for others that your life will touch. Use this as a point of reference or tuck it in the back of your mind.

Priscilla C. Baldwin

Priscilla C. Baldwin is a native of Pensacola, Florida. She is a mother of six adult children, and she has six grandchildren. She is the founder and CEO of "Total Care Agency" which was established in 2003 as Homemaker/Companion Services. Our name changed in 2012 to "Life Care Companions of Northwest Florida." The company's mission is to provide new concepts and innovative ideas about health-care in Northwest Florida. Priscilla has 15 years' experience in the mental health field as a Certified Behavior Technician, teaching behavior modification and conflict resolution. She continually receives training while working with Persons with Disabilities. Priscilla has additional experience and training working with adults, the elderly, and children, also providing Respite and Alzheimer Care. In addition, she has training in Alzheimer Patient Level 1 and Level 2 Assisted Living Facility in association with West Florida Hospital, Memory Disorder Clinic, and the Department of Elder Affairs. She received training as Infant Massage Instructor (IAIM) Nursing Assistant at Pensacola Junior College and as a Medical Assistant (Advanced Career Training NYC).

Priscilla obtained her certification as a Certified Administrator Assisted Living Facilities at University of South Florida/ Department of Elder Affairs. She is also a Certified Trainer in "Positive Approach Care" with Teepa Snow, educating care partners, families, staff, and other health care professionals in Dementia Care.

Contact Priscilla:
Website: /www.lifecarecompanionsnwfl.com
Facebook: www.facebook.com/priscillabaldwin

CHAPTER 12
Unstuck from Emotional Eating and Food Addiction
Noreen N. Henry

Have you been stuck in circumstances not knowing what to do or not even being aware that you are stuck?

Well, one of the circumstances I was stuck in was the cycle of emotional eating and food addiction. I say one of the cycles because I was stuck in more than one, but today my focus will be on being stuck in the emotional eating and food addiction cycle.

I know my journey is not unique. Like many, I have wrestled with emotional eating and food addiction for years, unable to be free from their bondage.

Yes, I had become addicted to food that started with emotional eating. I had an eating disorder. Never in my dreams did I think I would have an eating disorder.

Until I learned why I was using food for comfort, I continued in the vicious cycle of it and started developing bad eating habits.

I hope my story empowers those that have similar issues to break the cycle and become unstuck from it.

Note: More that 5% of the population may suffer from food addiction, according to one study. Food addiction occurs in almost 7% in women and 3% in men. Food addiction occurs in 2% of under/normal weight people and 8% of overweight/obese people. ("Food Addiction" psychguides.com)

The Beginning

It was hard to believe that I had an issue with food, let alone not knowing that emotional eating and food addiction was such a thing.

All the years I had struggled and was in bondage with food, I never thought that I had an issue. I had to accept the fact that I had a problem with food.

On top of the emotional eating and food addiction issues, one of the side effects is increased weight on the body, ugh. Even though I didn't like that I was gaining excess weight, it didn't stop the issues I had with food.

For years, I struggled to lose the weight that I had gained because of emotional eating that progressed to food addiction. I was abusing food and eating my feelings. I wasn't enjoying food the way it should be enjoyed. The thing is I didn't know that I was using food to fill a void. I wasn't aware of how unhappy I was.

I was using food for comfort to fill a void in my life, and that void was unhappiness. You see, it all started when something was wrong, something that I was unhappy about. The time I remember that I started eating emotionally was when my former husband and I were having a discussion. I don't remember what the discussion was, but I do know that that is when I started eating emotionally. It was a conversation that I wasn't happy with.

When the emotional eating started, as I have mentioned, I began to gain weight. I had to buy the next size up, then the next size up, then the next size up. I was embarrassed about being overweight.

When I first started gaining weight, I would cut out the labels in my clothes so no one could see the size I was wearing, not thinking that the size I had become can still be seen anyway, ugh. I somehow believed that removing the labels from the clothes to hide the size of my clothing wouldn't show my real size, the size I had become. I didn't want anyone to see the size of my clothing, ugh. I was embarrassed and I was ashamed, and even though I was embarrassed and ashamed of my body being bigger than I wanted it to be, I still continued to eat emotionally and still struggled to lose the weight. I was embarrassed to be bigger than what I wanted my body size to be and was not happy with the size I had become.

Yet, I still struggled to get off the excess weight I had gained. *Why?* I didn't know because I didn't understand that internal issues were the problem and played a big part in it.

Anyhow, I stopped removing the labels from my clothes and began trying to hide behind clothes by wearing things like jackets all the time, even though the size of my body was clearly seen, even though the size I allowed myself to get to could still be seen whether I hid it or not. It really didn't matter what I wore because the size of my body could still be seen. I was hiding because I was embarrassed, embarrassed that my body size was too large and that I had lost control.

I had developed a weight problem due to the emotional eating issue that is really overeating.

Over the years, I tried diet after diet to lose the weight I had gained to only lose then gain it back, because I had lost control and had a terrible issue with food. I had developed a wrong relationship with food. With dieting, the restrictions tend to cause bondage to addictions to food cravings. You crave for the foods that you can't have on the diet. This was another thing that added to the cycle of overeating.

I am known in my family to love chocolate. When I was on a diet, chocolate would be a forbidden food, and with it being forbidden, I would crave it. When I would go to the store, I would buy chocolate that's on sale and say things like "This is the last time I'm buying chocolate (not realistic, I know), since I am starting my diet tomorrow," or "One more time won't hurt." But the one more time continued to be one more time again and again, so the cycle continued and didn't end. This went on for a lot of years.

I am happy to say that I am delivered from the food cravings. It was in gaining the right knowledge and applying the knowledge that helped me to break the cravings cycle.

Anyhow, I couldn't hide the weight issue. To me, the struggle was obvious, and people didn't understand that I had an eating disorder so they would say things to me like, "Just don't eat," "You need to lose weight," and "What's wrong with you, what's the issue," "Just lose the weight already." The thing is, they didn't really know that there was a reason for the struggle and being stuck. At the time, I didn't know either. I didn't know I was stuck.

With these things being said to me, I felt more embarrassed and ashamed but continued in the cycle of being stuck in emotional eating and food addiction. No one knew how much I was struggling inside, I suffered in silence.

I have found that people in general often don't realize that there is a deeper, internal problem going on that result in struggles, and in my case, the struggle was with overeating food and my weight, and people typically are unaware of how hurtful their words about someone else's weight can be. Speaking for myself, I know I need to lose the weight, but I don't need to be told. I don't need to hear things like, "Boy, you got fat," or "You put on a lot of weight." It doesn't make me feel good to hear that. It will make me not want to be around anyone. But hey, until people walk in your shoes, most times, they won't understand.

When I was eating emotionally, I didn't know that it was an issue, and I didn't know there was a name for it until many years after I had begun this horrid journey. Horrid for me because it was a battle I was stuck in for years.

It started subtly too. I remember that I was eating when something was wrong, when it was an unhappy situation.

When I first started gaining weight, I didn't know:

*I was eating more
*why I was eating larger portions
*that I was eating emotionally, or that there was a name for it
*that I was eating more food because I was unhappy
*that it was an internal issue
*that I had developed food addiction
*that I had developed gluttony
*that I had become a mindless eater
*that I had become a binge eater
*that external things like other people, television, radio, etc. helped to shape the badly developed behaviors associated with emotional eating.
*why I couldn't break the bad habits
*that I needed outside help.

It was quite a while before I realized it was an issue because the habits that I had created were mindless, the subtlety. This is when it had progressed to food addiction.

There was a time I was embarrassed to talk about the extra weight on my body. In fact, I didn't talk about it at all, but I did do many diets. Very few knew that I wasn't happy with the size I had allowed my body to become, I hid it well. It was not something I thought about or realized how much I had hidden it. The masks we will wear, ugh.

It feels so good to be free to talk about it now.

In my opinion, society sets guidelines that are not healthy or are a reality for us, especially in the diet industry. Society has us thinking that it is better to be skinny.

Another opinion is that society portrays that you aren't good enough or healthy if you are fat. I know skinny people that are not healthy, and that goes to show that it is not always to do with your size that makes you healthy. I'm a healthy person, and I'm not on any medications. The only thing my doctor says to me is about the excess weight, to get it down.

Throughout my life, I've realized that people, in general, think that you are better when you are smaller in body size, meaning you only look good if you are skinny.

It's sad that when people that were overweight lose weight, you will hear things said like "You look good." My question to that is didn't they look good before?

In my experience, people make it seem that if you are overweight, something is wrong with you, and this is sad. We are all human, we all have or had some kind of struggle with something, cigarettes, drugs, alcohol, etc., but they are not looked down upon as much as someone with excess weight. I know because I have experienced this for many years. When people see me dressed up, and all glamorized, they say things like "You look good" and have a surprised look on their faces. This is not encouraging and needs to stop.

One sad thing I didn't like was when I was in a conversation with one of my sons one day. He said to me, "You're supposed to eat when something is wrong." He was a teenager at the time. I believe he learned this from watching me. We become what we are around. (It's so important who we are around with, and who we surround ourselves with. But that topic is for another time 😊).

One of the years I was having my annual physical, the doctor said to me that I had been gaining 5 lbs. a year. He asked me if I'm depressed, and I said "No." I said "no" because I didn't know that something was wrong internally.

Me, I was never happy being overweight. I was good with myself, always taking classes for personal development, reading, and taking courses in order to change my life, to make it better, but still, I had a struggle with food.

I've grown a lot in maturity over the years through gaining the right knowledge, but I was still not happy with the excess weight on my body. I just kept living and doing, always believing that I will obtain my weight loss goal or sometimes thinking that I'll never reach my goal, a fear and lie that I have yet to overcome. In all this, when my daughter was a teenager, she would tell me I don't look bad. That felt good to hear even though I still struggled.

I am happy to be working on myself in all ways to overcome all the negativity that has gone on in my life. I handle myself and my life much better with the right knowledge that I have been gaining.

When the Food Addiction Came About

As I touched on earlier, it was a summer evening that I began to eat more because something was wrong, I was not happy about something.

I clearly remember sitting in my kitchen on my second-floor apartment, sitting on the dining room chair next to my refrigerator, talking to the father of my children, and this is the point that I started eating more food because of what was going on (emotional eating).

I didn't realize that I was eating because of unhappiness. And at that time, I didn't know there was a name for what I was doing. I had created a pattern, a cycle of overeating.

It didn't help that the father of my children started saying things to me like, "You see food, and you eat it." At first, I thought he was telling me a joke, then I realized he was referring to me. He would also say, "You're once, twice, three times a lady," and "If you don't lose the weight, I will leave you." We were taking a trip to Jamaica, and he would say "You better lose weight because everyone in Jamaica is skinny," among other things.

Do you think the things being said to me helped me?

Do you think the things being said made me lose weight?

Nope, you are right, it didn't help at all. In fact, it made things worse. I felt even worse about myself, and it was all internal because I didn't show it on the outside or so I thought.

People tend to battle with things internally in silence because no one knows they have an internal battle going on even for years. I know this because I was once there.

The things that were said to me made me feel bad about myself even more so because I was already feeling bad due to the weight gain.

People really don't know and understand how much damage their negative words will cause. I never used to understand the importance of our words either until I got the revelation that our words frame our world. Whatever we say will come to pass. We must be so careful of the words we speak and even what we think about (this will be delved into in another book 😊).

No one understood the struggle. No one understood the bondage I was in. I didn't even understand it myself. It bothered me a great deal to be overweight, but no one knew that. I kept it in my mind, and it showed up on my body.

Reasons Why I Want to Be Rid of the Excess Fat

- I want to please my Creator.
- I don't want to hide anymore.
- I want to be back at the weight where I am comfortable with my body size.
- I don't want to be labeled as fat, unhealthy, or have no discipline or control.
- I want to be showing up right for me.
- I want to wear smaller clothing sizes.
- I don't want to shop in the plus-size section of the store anymore.

- I want to be my authentic self with my body size.
- And the most important one, I want to properly value myself the way the Most High intended.

It is commitment, work, and persistence to get the excess weight off, along with getting educated (the right knowledge) on the causes of eating disorders to get to the root of the problem so that when all the excess weight is gone, it will be gone forever. Unlearning and relearning coping skills, instead of eating.

Side Effects

Some of the other side effects I experienced, apart from the weight gain, were:

- Low self-esteem
- Mild depression
- Feelings of insecurity
- Feeling sad, hopeless, and despair
- Increased irritability
- Emotional detachment or numbness
- Not wanting to go out due to my size, wanting to avoid social events

I struggled with many things, not believing that I had struggled with this battle of trying to lose weight for more than 25 years, wow!

Sometimes I would think to myself, how did I allow myself to gain so much weight? I had gotten a little over 100+ lbs. excess weight which is too much weight for height.

I would think thoughts of not being small again. I now know that this is based on fear, the fear of not being my ideal size again.

There are times that I didn't want to go to a social function because of my body size, but I would chump it up and go anyway, with no one knowing what I was dealing with. The mask is so real, acting like everything is fine when it isn't.

I would think, what are others thinking about the extra fat on my body, like it matters 😊. I guess it mattered to me because of knowing how people will think and how society projects people with extra weight on their bodies.

As I mentioned before, people would say things to me like, "Just lose the weight," or "Do you exercise?", not knowing that I was already feeling bad about myself for not weighing what I used to weigh before gaining the extra weight.

We need to understand that if someone is not their ideal weight, in my opinion, there is an internal issue going on that needs to be addressed, dealt with, and corrected. Getting to the root of the problem so that it can be fixed, and not only fixed, but fixed for good.

More Things I Would Think

For job interviews, I would think, "I have to lose weight first before going on job interviews." I know I would say this because society dictates you must be skinny. Don't believe me, look at the TV and see the number of women that are skinny in them.

That I'm not adequate enough.

When taking pictures, let me make sure to stand a certain way to not show my true size.

With a function like a wedding, I would think about making plans to lose weight before it.

The things that overweight people will think and deal with are quite alarming. It's actually disturbing. You can read more of my story in my book *Food Addiction: The Struggle Has Been Real.*

The Cycles

I was in the diet cycle that started in my mid-teens
I was in the emotional eating cycle that started in my late 20s.
I was in the binge eating, mindless eating, bad habit eating, etc. cycle I had developed with emotional eating.

A lot of cycles to be stuck in, ugh.

I have done binge-eating, etc., and the thing is, after all these years of diet after diet, you would think I'd have been delivered from the eating disorder cycle, but no. It took me getting counseling many years later to overcome the eating disorder.

As I always say, you have to do something different or nothing changes. In fact, it gets worse, and in this case, the bad eating disorder. Counselors or coaches are a big help when you have the right one. I say the right one because at one time I had a counselor that gave advice and things got worse.

How I Overcame

Firstly, I had to be aware that something was wrong to do something about it. When I learned about emotional eating, I began reading books about it. This is what helped me to overcome emotional eating.

3 Quick Tips to Overcoming Emotional Eating/Food Addiction

1. Stop, think, and answer questions like: What's going on in your life now that's making you want to eat? What emotion are you experiencing? Will eating make you feel better? Will eating solve the problem?
2. Put boundaries in place. For example, if a particular food will trigger you, keep it out of your home.
3. Get help. It was in seeking help that helped me to overcome. For me, I started seeing help with books, then after a while, I got counseling.

Today, I continue on my journey. I haven't gotten rid of the excess weight yet, but I am determined to and will get there. I have been unlearning and relearning. I have an overcomer course that is geared to help undo wrong habits, and it has been enhanced to include even more. I look forward to sharing that.

I had been seeing a grief counselor and after a while, I started speaking about the weight issue. She suggested I read a book called *Intuitive Eating* and said that she will help me with it. Upon reading this book, I got delivered from cravings. I can go to the store, look at chocolate, and not buy it because I don't want it anymore. It is such a good feeling to be set free from the cravings because that had been a battle for years. Emotional eating and dieting cause much more than emotional eating. My overcomer program will now include aspects of this as I am revamping my program to include a healthier way of eating. Shifting the mindset about dieting, I am so happy to have overcome the battle to be on my journey for my ideal body size. I am happy to not be an emotional eater anymore, not crave foods I couldn't have anymore, not become addicted to food anymore, and all the other things that come along with food addiction.

If you are reading this and have been stuck in the wrong relationship with food, you too can become unstuck from it.

Victorious living, it's possible!

Noreen N. Henry

Noreen N. Henry is a Victorious Living Strategist who is focused on living victoriously, living her best life now, and creating victorious habits for the life of your dreams. She is known for her knowledge, wisdom, and understanding along with instant results. One of her passions is transforming women's lives from defeat, mediocrity, and brokenness to victory. She is a powerful coach, international speaker, trainer, author, and health educator. She is an eight-time #1 international best-seller who published 24 books.

Noreen experienced many adversities that led to her learning tools to be victorious. As a result, Noreen founded Victorious Living Culture, a movement where her products and services help countless individuals turn their situations into victory and into their God-given life's purpose.

Noreen's native residence is London, England. She migrated to the States in her late teens. She came from humble beginnings in a small town in East London and has progressed so much so that she was graced to be on a billboard on Broadway in Times Square, New York City. She never dreamed she would be on a billboard, let alone in the heart of New York City.

Noreen obtained an AAS degree and various certificates and diplomas. Noreen is an avid reader who continues to educate herself. She is currently enrolled in International School of Ministry's Bachelor's degree program. Noreen completed the Cornell's Women's Entrepreneur program and AmplifyHER Voice Speaker & Mentorship Certification Program. She continues to take courses to craft her talents.

Noreen is an ordained minister and is a certified Biblical Counselor. She is a member of the American Association of Christian Counselors, 4 Corners Alliance, John Maxwell Team Member, Toastmasters International, and Promote-Her. Noreen is also certified in Administrative Assistance, Cake Baking, Decorating, Biblical Counseling, and GSC. She has acquired "Another Seat at the Table: Inclusion and Diversity Compliance License."

Noreen has been featured on Gratitude Girls, Authors in Business, National Black Book Festival, Visions of Greatness Entrepreneur Spotlight, Conversations with Lady Linda, Kingdom Purpose Talk, Courageous Woman Magazine, SNAPD Downtown Toronto, AmplifyHer Magazine, Divine Purpose Magazine, and various other media outlets. Some of Noreen's work has been seen on CBS, ABC, FOX, NBC, and The CW. She created the "Unleash Your Greatest Potential, Living Your Best Life NOW! Annual Event and now has a TV talk show called "Victorious Living With Noreen" because "Stuck Is NOT Your Story."

Noreen is passionate about victorious living and cares a great deal about mankind. She is making the world a better place one person at a time. The song "People Help the People" was dedicated to Noreen by one of her nieces.

Noreen is the mother of three children, and she has four grandchildren. She resides in New York City. Reach Noreen on www.NoreenNHenry.com or at Victorious Living Culture's academy www.StartYourVictoriousLife.com

The Mission of

"STUCK IS NOT YOUR STORY"

First, this project is at the leading of our Divine Creator for a series of "Stuck Is NOT Your Story" to show that you are not alone in your "stuck," place and that you can change, it is possible to overcome and be victorious.

It is Victorious Living Culture's mission to provide you with hope. To encourage, inspire, and motivate people all around the world, through the power of overcoming and victorious stories, to help you be on your journey of your best life NOW!

As it is with mankind, because no one is exempt, we all go through circumstances that cause us to be stuck. One of the things I was stuck in was emotional eating that progressed to unhealthy eating habits. It was a struggle for many years which is why Victorious Living Culture's "Stuck Is NOT Your Story" is important to make a global impact with helping you become unstuck.

Victorious Living Culture's

Products & Services

One-to-One Coaching

www.calendly.com/noreennhenry

****

Victorious Living Culture's Academy

Victorious Living Community – Free Resources

30-Day Journey of Foundational Tips For Victorious Living

Victorious Living Kit

Stuck Is NOT Your Story: Becoming Aware

Post Live Event: "Overcomer Course" Stuck Is NOT Your Story:

Don't Allow Food To Rob You Of Your Life

A Secret To Success Is Our Thoughts & Words

Plus many more to come…

Register here: www.StartYourVictoriousLife.com

****

Published Books

Are You In God's Will Or Not? Do You Know That You Have to Choose?

Victorious Living: Guide To A Happier Life

Legacy Journal: Thoughts For A Better Life

Food Addiction: The Struggle Has Been Real

A Legacy Book: Interesting Facts Journal

Born Again, Now What?

T-shirts / Canvas Bags

Plus more…

www.NoreenNHenry.com/shop

Acknowledgements

Andrea Briscoe

- Alecia Brown
- Anthony McKinney
- Bernard McPherson
- Bishop Edward A. Coles
- Edna Faye Blackwell
- Evangelist Armitcher Delaney (My Godmommy)
- Greg Wilcox
- Ina Dean
- Ivan Beauchamps
- Janice Brunson
- Javacia Stukes
  J&L Stukes Travel Agency

- Jolita Renae Pennix
- Kiaira Brown
- Kim Hines
- Kimberly Gibson
  Cambrae Business Strategies, Inc

- L. Renee Nix
  The L Renee Way

- Lady Marie Moye
  Lady Marie Creations

- Louise Jackson
- Mary Caison
- Mary Coleman
- Mary Glass
- Mother Vanessa Partin
  In The Know Consulting

- Nettie Johnson
- Nicole Ward
- Robert Bates
- Rudy Briscoe
- Shalita Briscoe Simmons
- Sharon M Holmes
- Stephanie & Mike Woolard
- Veronica Hardy

Carol M. Quigless

- Charlotte Hirsch You
- Denise White Harrison-Johnson
  Denise's H.O.P.E. Ministry

- Doris Stith
- Linda Tharrington Goines
- Mike Stanley
- Sharon Hughes Taylor
- Susan Kumar

Dr. JoWanda Rollins-Fells

- Antonio Clinkscales
  avclinkscales@msn.com
  Life Way Services, LLC

- Bishop Arthur N. Werts & Minister Saundra Werts
  wertsministries@verizon.net
  Werts Ministries

- Bishop Darryl
  bishopdfhusband@gmail.com
  Campaign For The Kingdom

- Bishop Earl Dudley
  edudley79@yahoo.com
  Right Way Apostolic Church Of God

- Brenda Ring Wood
  brendaringwood@gmail.com
  Becoming The Best You

- David & Rayna Dudley
  syf633.brand@gmail.com
  Seek Ye First Clothing

- Dr. Philicia Jefferson
  dr.pjefferson@gmail.com
  National Christian Counselor Institute, The Call To Counsel

- Felisha W. Battle
  fefeinc@icloud.com
  The Go Live Experience

- Jessie Rollins
  jessienjd@yahoo.com
  MeMa's CubHouse

- Joy Hill
  joyah1106@gmail.com
  Luvncare

- Kathy Wilson
  kathy.wilson@taggedyouth.org
  TAGGED

- Kelisha Worrell
  kw@kelishaworrell.com
  United Destiny Institute

- Pastor De'Rain F. Irvin
  3n1min@gmail.com
  3N1 Ministries, LLC

- Pastor Devolus D. Parker
  agapefamilylife@gmail.com
  Agape Family Life Church

- Prophet Keith Douglas
  kdoug716@gmail.com
  The Prophet's Corner

- Prophetess Joanne Walker
  j.walkerpurple1@gmail.com
  God Got It Ministry

- Rev. Dr. LaMont E. Wimbish, Sr.
  lewshand224@gmail.com
  That Ye May Know

- Rev. Pennie Stallworth
  pennmaelpan@gmail.com
  PennMael Information For Life

- Swehla Hunt
  totaldiscoveries4u@gmail.com
  The Epic You TV Show

Joy Green

- Anthony W Ruffin
- Barbara Wortham
- Brandy McCall
- Brett Moye
- Carie Cordia Campbell Thomas
- Chuck McDaniels Jr
  Curaleaf

- Clark Adams
- Faith McAlister
- Helynn Boughner
- Isabel Diaz
- Jai Brown
- Jenea Floyd
- Joy LaBelle
  Joy Unleash Ur Potential, LLC

- Lu Moore
  LuMales Tamales

- Maajida Muhammad
- Tiffany Williams-Parra
  Phoenix Fitness Fanatics

Latika Vines

- Cassandra Conley
- Cime Eklund
- Clay Simpson
- Cori Simpson
- Crystal Braxton
- Dominique Dewel
- Fernandez Vines
- Melva Thompson
- Monique Martinez
- Nelda Jackson
- Roy Hill, Jr
- Simone Braxton

Lynnecia S. Eley

- Annie M. Brown
- Beverly Williams
- Calvin Eley
- CJ Eley
- Cynthia Barnes
- Denise Mills Mincey

- Elizabeth Blue
- Gloria Denson
- Gregory Russell
- Jazie Barnes
- Karen Edmond
- Karen Piner
- Katrina Clear
- Marable Gabriel
- Patricia Varone
- Paul Blackman
- Terri Johnson
- Trenice J. Brinkley
  Two Queens Media

Marilyn Green

- Anna M. Bell
- Arnetta McNeese Bailey
- Audra Baker
- Catina Lynett Rupert
- Domino Angelica Marie Williams
- Erica Brown Gayles
- Gertte H. Smith
- Jeanine Watson
- JoAnn Rankins-Cannon
- John Andrew Williams, III
- KIM KELLY-DAVIS
- Madame White
- Matthew Alexander Williams
- Mechelle Jones
- Nicolle S. Thompson-Williams
- Shante Smith-Daniels
- Soledad Amelia Joy Williams

Nicole Rhone

- Corey Mandley

- Darius Rhone
- Deborah Arana
- Dr. Shakesha M. Costict, PhD, LMHC, NCC, CMHS
- Gillian D Hill
  Note With Integrity

- Jeremiah Mandley
- Katrice Cloyd
- Kristy Kotek
  Roosevelt University

- Melinda Martinez-Epperson
  The Play Lab

- Samantha Washington
- Sonya Iyasere
- Tamika McTier
  Ageless Conversations LLC

- Tonychia Clark-Weary
- Yanni Profit
  Business Manager Chic llc

Noreen N. Henry

- Angela Tate
  Caregiver Life Coach Angela Amazin Tate
  A.amazingpower@gmail.com
  @iamcoachamazin

- Dr. Michelle Davenport
  sistermcb@msn.com

- Jennifer Niu
  Figwisdomwellness@gmail.com
  Faith In God, LLC

- Nadine Fortune BSN RN
  fortunatelivingrn@gmail.com
  @fortunateliving

- Dwight D. Furguson
  ddfurguson@gmail.com
  @ddfurguson

- Terryann Smith
  annterry173@gmail.com
  @Sweettee731

- Margaret Green
  Protecting yourself and your family
  mhgreen50@gmail.com
  @Health_isalsowealth

Shontae Horton

- Audrey Hardy
- Carol Marcus Connor
- Crystal Merritt-Ching
  crystalching46@yahoo.com
  Think Goodness

- Jeffrey R Hardy
  tajmuzik@aol.com
  Jireh Roses

- Jennifer Clark
- Qimmah Crawford-Wright
- Richard Hardy

Tracey Ford

- Angela Evans
- Anthea Appiah
- Barbara F. Murphy

- Calvin T. Stanford
- Chivaughnn Smith
- Courtni Boyd
- Dee Young
- Derrick Thompson
- Dwayne Wyatt
- Faydria Fox
- Fred "Flash" Tisdale
- Justina Ford
- Kaileigha Jordan
- Kathrine Lim
- Kimberly Jackson
- LaChrista Walter
- Latonya Cato-Owens
- Linda Hodge
- Marian Pierson
- Michele Cato
- Neisha Cannon
- Nina Trevino
- Raynell Steward aka Supa Cent
- Rhonda Greer
- Shannon Alece aka Comedian Shannon
- Sharon Sterling
- Steven Morgan aka Luizana Cash
- Suhayla Sabir
- Terri Williams
- Wanja Mitchell

Made in the USA
Middletown, DE
26 October 2022